Reform of the House of Lords

MANCHESTER
1824

Manchester University Press

POCKET POLITICS

Pocket politics presents short, pithy summaries of complex topics on socio-political issues both in Britain and overseas. Academically sound, accessible and aimed at the interested general reader, the series will address a subject range including political ideas, economics, society, the machinery of government and international issues. Unusually, perhaps, authors are encouraged, should they choose, to offer their own conclusions rather than strive for mere academic objectivity. The series will provide stimulating intellectual access to the problems of the modern world in a user-friendly format.

Reform of the House of Lords

Philip Norton

Manchester University Press

Published by Manchester University Press
Altrincham Street, Manchester M1 7JA

www.manchesteruniversitypress.co.uk

British Library Cataloguing-in-Publication Data
A catalogue record for this book is available from the British Library

ISBN   978 1 5261 1923 0   paperback

First published 2017

Typeset
by Toppan Best-set Premedia Limited
Printed in Great Britain
by CPI Group (UK) Ltd, Croydon, CR0 4YY

Contents

Tables

Why the House of Lords matters

THE United Kingdom has a parliamentary system of government. Government is not elected directly (as in a presidential system), but is chosen through parliamentary elections. A party achieving an absolute majority of seats in the House of Commons is invited to form the government. Political parties seeking to implement their preferred programme of public policy therefore fight to win seats. The chamber of the House of Commons is the arena in which the second-largest party forms an official Opposition and in which it, and other parties, question and challenge government. The chamber provides the Opposition with the opportunity to demonstrate that it is the alternative government, ready to replace the party opposite at the next election. The exchanges between the Prime Minister and the Leader of the Opposition at the weekly Prime Minister's Question Time act as a magnet for the television cameras.

Given the centrality of the House of Commons to political life in the United Kingdom, it is not unusual to see Parliament and the House of Commons treated as synonymous terms. Commentators will variously say 'Parliament today is debating ...' when they mean 'The House of Commons today is debating ...'. The focus on the House of Commons is not surprising, but masks the fact that the United Kingdom has a bicameral, that is a two-chamber, legislature. The House of Lords is the second chamber of Parliament.

As a second chamber, the House of Lords is distinctive for three reasons. The first is the very fact of its existence as a second chamber. Most nations – almost two-thirds – have unicameral, that is single-chamber, legislatures (Massicotte 2001). Bicameral legislatures tend to be a feature of federal nations. However, they are also to be found in some unitary, often large nations, such as France, Italy, and the UK. The House of Lords' second distinctive feature is to be found in its origins and its longevity. As with the House of Commons, there was no specific date on which we can say it came into existence. It has evolved and, as we shall see (Chapter 2), has done so over several centuries. The third distinctive feature is that the members of the House are not elected. In this, the House is not unique. Several nations, including Canada, have appointed second chambers (see Russell 2000: 30). However, the fact that it is not elected is important for shaping the contemporary relationship between the two chambers. By virtue of being the elected chamber, the House of Commons enjoys primacy. The fact that members of the House of Lords are not elected is core also to understanding the debate on reform of the House.

Until the early twentieth century, the two chambers were for most purposes co-equal, but the growth of a mass electorate established the supremacy of the elected chamber and the House of Lords lost its capacity to veto the wishes of the House of Commons. The first half of the twentieth century saw measures to limit the power of the House and the second half saw measures to change its composition. Although the nature of the membership of the House of Lords has changed substantially, it remains an unelected House. It is derided by critics as undemocratic and as a relic of a feudal era.

What, then, is the point of the House of Lords? The House of Lords matters: firstly, because Parliament matters, and secondly, because within Parliament it fulfils tasks which it sees as adding value to the political process. The House conceives its role as not to conflict with but, rather, to complement the work of the House of Commons. We address here what the House presently does and who fulfils the work, that is, the membership. How the House got to where it is we address in the next chapter and what *should* happen to it in later chapters.

Importance of Parliament

Parliament matters because politics matters. Politics is the peaceful resolution of disputes as to the policy to apply to a particular population. Parliament provides the authoritative forum for the different sides to be heard and, crucially, has to give its assent in order for measures of public policy to be binding. The doctrine of parliamentary sovereignty asserts that the outputs of Parliament – that is, Acts of Parliament – are supreme and can be set aside by no body other than Parliament itself (Dicey 1885: 39–40). The courts and law-enforcement agencies enforce Acts of Parliament. However popular a policy is, it cannot be enforced as law until approved by Parliament.

A party securing an absolute majority of seats at a general election will form the government and normally be able to achieve the outcomes it wants, but it still has to draw up bills to implement its programme. Those bills have to go through Parliament and the rules and processes of each House create important constraints (Norton 2001). Enacting legislation is time consuming; a bill has to go through one House and then the other, with several stages in each, and time for considering bills within each parliamentary session (which usually lasts one year) is limited. With certain exceptions, bills that are not passed by the end of the session fail. Government has to be selective in determining which measures to bring forward and each will normally be subject to sustained scrutiny. From an institutional perspective, Parliament is thus a powerful body (Norton 2013: 6–7). Often, the key consideration for government business managers is not whether they have the votes to pass a measure, but whether they have the time to get it through. The legislative process is based on the premise that government is entitled to get its business considered, but the Opposition has a right to be heard.

Functions of the House of Lords

Parliament as an institution, then, matters: it is core to the nation's political system. What, then, of the role of the House of Lords within Parliament? The functions ascribed principally to parliamentary second chambers are those of representation and reflection (Norton 2007a: 6–8). In federal nations, for example, second chambers are created to represent the component states or districts. The House of Lords is not a representative chamber in terms of being elected and speaking for a particular body of people, nor is it representative in terms of being socially typical (Pitkin 1967). Its contribution is in terms of reflection: that is, deliberating, particularly but not exclusively, on what the first chamber has done. As a reflective chamber, its contribution can be divided into several functions. We treat its functions as consequences for the political system, in other words, what it actually does, rather than tasks formally ascribed to it.

The functions derive from the House's seeking to complement and not challenge the work of the elected chamber. The House seeks to add value to the political process, including by carrying out work that the Commons may not have the time, the political will, or the resources (such as time) to fulfil. The three most significant are *legislative scrutiny*, *calling government to account*, and *debate*. The three are not mutually exclusive, but they are analytically separable.

The most important is *legislative scrutiny* (Norton 2016: 117–36). Most time in the chamber – 50 to 60 per cent each session – is given over to considering legislation, mostly legislation brought forward by government. Legislative scrutiny is also the function that has the most impact, affecting substantially the content of law. Bills have to go through the same stages in each House (see Table 1.1), but there are differences in terms of procedures and focus.

The House of Commons has limited time and it now timetables bills through the use of programme motions, which stipulate the times at which particular parts of a bill must be concluded. Sections of a bill not reached for debate when time runs out receive no debate. The Commons tends to focus on the principle of a bill and on the politically contentious provisions. The Opposition may force a vote on the second reading (in other words, the

Table 1.1   Legislative stages in each House

First reading	Formal introduction. Title is read out.
Second reading	Debate on principle.
Committee	Consideration of amendments and approval of each clause, either in a committee away from the chamber (public bill committee in Commons; grand committee – which any member can attend – in the Lords) or in committee of the whole House.
Report	Bill returns to chamber, where further amendments, usually on issues not resolved in committee, are considered; proceedings are more formal and limited than at committee stage.
Third reading	Final approval of bill by the House. In the Commons, usually taken straight after report and often without debate; in the Lords, gap of at least three days after report stage and further amendments may be considered.
Commons'/Lords' amendments	Consideration by House in which bill originated of any amendments made by the other House. Both Houses have to agree for bill to proceed to Royal Assent. If there is disagreement, amendments may go back and forth between the two ('ping pong') until agreement is reached.

principle) of a bill and then, when the bill goes to committee for detailed consideration, will focus on particularly contentious provisions or on particular amendments that it has tabled (see Russell, Morris and Larkin 2013: 27–8). The purpose is to highlight the deficiencies of the bill and the alternative proposals of the Opposition.

In the House of Lords, the focus is the detail of the bill. By convention, the House does not seek to reject on second (or third) reading any measure promised in the government party's election manifesto, and in practice it does not usually vote on the second reading of any bill that forms part of the government's programme. It will debate the bill, but accepts that the elected chamber, the House of Commons, is entitled to get its way in terms of the ends of the bill. It therefore focuses on means rather than ends. Time is devoted to detailed scrutiny. This is facilitated by the fact that the House does not make use of programme motions. All provisions of a bill are therefore considered. Also, unlike in the Commons, all amendments that are tabled by peers are considered. (In the Commons, there is a selection by the Speaker in the House or the chair in committee of amendments to be debated.) The Lords also has an additional stage at which to consider amendments. Both Houses utilise committee and report stages for considering amendments. The Commons uses third reading (often taken formally) for the final approval of a bill: no amendments are considered. In the Lords, however, amendments can be, and variously are, taken at third reading to resolve issues not resolved at preceding stages.

The Lords' detailed scrutiny has notable consequences for legislation. Each year, some hundreds, and sometimes a few thousand, amendments to government bills are secured in the House of Lords. 'Almost all observers agree that the quality of peers' work is usually high and the outcomes useful', wrote Emma Crewe. 'They give more time to scrutiny than MPs and make a huge number of improvements to Bills: 2,557 amendments in 2001–02 and 2,996 in 2002–03' (Crewe 2005: 195). The record was set in the 1999–2000 session, when 4,761 amendments were achieved.

Most of the amendments made in the Lords – more than 90 per cent – are proposed by the government (Shell 2007: 100) and so, not surprisingly, they are accepted. This has led one authority on the Lords, Donald Shell, to describe the House as a 'convenience to the government' (Shell 2007: 126). However, this misses the point that the genesis of these amendments frequently lies not with government but with amendments moved by peers at earlier stages. It is not unusual for peers to move amendments at the detailed committee stage, for ministers to then say they will consider the matter, and for them to return at the report stage of a bill with a properly drafted government amendment.

A study by Russell of twelve government bills in the period from 2005 to 2012 found that a majority of substantive government amendments (55 per cent) could be traced to amendments moved earlier by peers, with others attributable to reports from committees or pressure from MPs (Russell 2013: 173). While the proportion is significant, it is some of the individual changes achieved to bills that can be the most important aspect of the impact of the House of Lords. It is not unusual for some bills to be virtually rewritten in the House of Lords, with ministers conceding that they have been much improved as a result. The House thus makes a difference to legislation, both in quantitative and in qualitative terms.

Three other dimensions of legislative scrutiny are particular to the House of Lords. The first is the scrutiny of proposals for European Union (EU) law. The Commons' European Scrutiny Committee examines each proposal against certain criteria, but undertakes no in-depth examination and makes no comments on the merits of the proposal. Whereas the Commons goes for breadth, the Lords goes for depth (Norton 1996: 96). The Lords' European Union Committee sifts the proposals to identify the more important ones and then examines these in some detail. The scrutiny is undertaken by one of six sub-committees, each with responsibility for particular sectors of public policy. The size and number of the sub-committees means that seventy or more members of the House are engaged in the detailed scrutiny of proposed EU law as well as wider developments within the EU. The committee's reports are sent not only to the UK government but also to the institutions of the EU, and have a reputation for being reasoned, evidence based, and authoritative.

Prior to the 23 June 2016 referendum in the UK on the UK's membership of the EU, the committee published a report examining the legal means by which the UK could withdraw from the EU (European Union Committee 2016a). Given the outcome, it will be centrally engaged in examining the government's negotiations for withdrawal (European Union Committee 2016b.)

Consideration of EU proposals is a form of pre-legislative scrutiny, considering measures before they are decided by the EU Council of Ministers and European Parliament. The second distinctive dimension of legislative scrutiny by the House is post-legislative scrutiny of UK law. Until well into the twenty-first century, neither House made any systematic attempt to check if Acts, once in force, achieved their intended purpose. In recent years, the Lords has set up at least one ad hoc committee each session (appointed for the lifetime of the session) to consider whether particular Acts of Parliament have met their purpose.

In the 2010–15 Parliament, committees were appointed to consider legislation dealing with adoption, public inquiries, mental health, and extradition. In the first session of the 2015 Parliament, a committee considered the disability provisions of the Equality Act 2010, and in the second session one was appointed to examine the Licensing Act 2003, which regulates the sale of alcohol. Additionally in 2015, a permanent committee, the Delegated Powers and Regulatory Reform Committee, reviewed the Legislative and Regulatory Reform Act 2006, which enables ministers to make orders to remove unnecessary regulations. The value of such review is to ensure that legislation is achieving what it is intended to achieve and, if not, to discuss with government ways in which it can be amended or different means of implementation can be adopted.

The third distinctive dimension is in the use of committees for scrutinising a different form of legislation, namely delegated legislation (that is, order-making powers conferred on a minister by an Act). One committee, the Delegated Powers and Regulatory Reform Committee, examines the order-making powers in a bill to ensure that the provision of parliamentary approval for such orders is appropriate. Another, the Secondary Legislation Scrutiny Committee, considers orders once they are brought forward by ministers and reports on any that have important political or legal implications or are defective, for example by achieving policy objectives inappropriately (Norton 2016: 126–7). Delegated legislation now constitutes a substantial body of law, both quantitatively and qualitatively, and the Lords' committees provide sustained examination for which there is no equivalent in the Commons (see Fox and Blackwell 2014).

The function of *calling government to account* encompasses both a reactive role, questioning and challenging government, and a proactive one, recommending action that may be taken by government. Like the House of Commons, the House of Lords provides an arena in which government is questioned and forced to justify its policies and actions. It employs similar means to the Commons – question time, committees, and floor debates – but operates in a way that seeks to complement what happens in the other House. This is especially the case with investigative committees.

Like the House of Commons, the House of Lords has moved from being a primarily chamber-oriented institution – most business being conducted on the floor of the House – to a more specialised body utilising committees. Although the Commons has, since the early twentieth century, regularly used committees for dealing with the detail of legislation, until relatively recently the Lords transacted most business, including legislation, on the floor of the House.

The House now makes use of its capacity to take business in grand committee, in effect a parallel chamber (meeting in the Moses Room, a large room close to the chamber), which any member can attend. The committee stage of some bills, especially those that are not contentious between the parties, is taken in grand committee. The use of this procedure is not so much a form of specialisation – given that any peer can attend – as a means of saving time in the chamber, enabling more business to be considered. Where the House has become more specialised is through the use of investigative select committees.

In the Commons, the emphasis in the use of investigative committees has been on, though not confined to, departmental select committees. There is a committee for each government department to examine the policy, administration, and expenditure of that department and associated public bodies. To avoid duplication, the Lords has appointed committees to cover cross-cutting issues, those not confined to a particular department. These comprise committees on Science and Technology, Communications, Economic Affairs, and the Constitution. The last of these has proved especially influential, with both government and the House, through its reports on bills and wider constitutional developments (Le Seuer and Simpson Caird 2013). There is also, as we have seen, the European Union Committee, working through six sub-committees. The Lords also joins with the Commons in a Joint Committee on Human Rights, which has helped to raise the profile of human rights in both Houses as well as engendering a rights-based culture within government departments (Hunt, Hooper and Yowell 2012).

These committees are permanent committees, reappointed at the start of each session. The House also makes use of temporary or ad hoc committees, appointed usually for the lifetime of a session. As we have noted, it uses ad hoc committees for post-legislative scrutiny. It also utilises them to examine particular issues. In the three sessions from 2014–15 to 2016–17, it appointed committees on affordable childcare, the Arctic, digital skills, social mobility, the built environment, sexual violence in conflict, charities, financial exclusion, and the long-term sustainability of the National Health Service.

Committee work complements scrutiny that takes place in the chamber. In addition to debates, the chamber is used for questioning ministers. As in the House of Commons, there is a daily question time at the start of the day's proceedings. It lasts for no more than thirty minutes and, unlike in the Commons, no more than four questions are taken (Norton 2013: 124–5).

This allows several minutes for each question, enabling peers from different sides of the House to put supplementary questions and allowing for a minister to be probed in some detail. Ministers will also make statements on current issues, each statement being followed by time for questions to the minister.

The function of *debate*, as we have seen, encompasses legislation (the House debates the principle and the specific provisions of bills), but also extends beyond it. There are opportunities for peers to raise and discuss issues that they wish to have discussed. Sometimes the initiative comes from government – to discuss, for example, a particular policy or action – but there are means for other peers to initiate debates. These include long, usually two-and-a-half hour, debates in the chamber, normally on Thursdays, and shorter, usually one-hour, debates in the chamber or grand committee. Peers may also generate debate through introducing private members' bills. Although these are legislative measures, they fall more under the heading of debate, since the reason for their introduction is not usually the expectation that they will the statute book. Very few private members' bills make it into law. Rather, they are introduced in order to generate debate and get a government response (see Natzler and Millar 1993: 190). They often constitute part of a campaign to generate support for what is in the bill, in the hope that a momentum will develop, leading eventually to government accepting the need for action.

The debates often fall outside the normal framework of party conflict and cover issues of concern to individuals and groups outside the House. They may cover issues as diverse as prison reform, tackling the problem of HIV/AIDS, international aid, drugs policy reform, sport, Commonwealth trade, animal welfare, parish churches, and encouraging voluntary associations. A number of subjects may be covered in the course of a day. On 26 May 2016, for example, there were two long debates in the chamber, one on special educational needs and disabilities in schools and the other on ensuring equal access to mental health and physical healthcare; in between the two there was a short debate on young voters in the EU referendum.

The debate function encompasses an agenda-setting role. Although many subjects of debate may have been considered before, some may be coming on to the parliamentary agenda for the first time. A good example is the Patient (Assisted Dying) Bill, a private member's bill introduced by Lord Joffe (by background a South African human rights lawyer) in 2003. The bill provided that, subject to certain safeguards, it is no longer a criminal offence to assist someone who is terminally ill and wishes to bring their life to a close. The bill helped to get the issue debated and constituted the start of a campaign to get the law changed. Assisted dying has remained a contentious social issue, with various Assisted Dying Bills introduced in later sessions, although none has as yet made it to the statute book.

These constitute the main functions fulfilled by the House. Their attribution to the House and the manner in which they are carried out have not given rise to significant controversy. They are viewed as worthwhile and generally well fulfilled. The House devotes considerable time to fulfilling them and, like the House of Commons, the House of Lords is one of the busiest legislative chambers in the world. However, unlike the House of Commons, the House is notable for the absence of a government majority. (Over 20 per cent of the membership comprise cross-bench peers, that is, peers with no party affiliation.) This, as we shall see, has been a feature of the House since 1999 and it has facilitated the House in carrying out its functions effectively. Most amendments are agreed without a vote, but if one does take place the government is not assured of victory. Knowing this, ministers have to take the House seriously and to engage with its members. To get a contested provision accepted, they have to work to carry others in the House beyond those in their own party ranks.

The result is that the House of Lords is notable for the politics of justification, unlike the House of Commons, which is characterised by the politics of assertion (Norton 2016). Ministers in the House of Commons can take an adversarial stance, knowing that they have a majority of MPs to support them. In the Lords, ministers do not have such a majority and so they tend to be more accommodating.

Membership of the Lords

Who, then, are the members of the House who carry out these tasks? The basis of membership has changed substantially since the late 1950s.

Until 1958, the House of Lords was composed almost wholly of hereditary peers (those who had inherited their titles, and consequently their seats in the House) and leading prelates of the established church, the Church of England. The former comprised what are known as the lords temporal and the latter the lords spiritual. The lords spiritual were, and remain, different from lords temporal in that they retire when they cease to be bishops. (They also form just a small part of the House, the number having been confirmed by statute in 1878 at twenty-six.) Hereditary peers sat for life, with their titles and seats in the House passing to their heirs. They were joined from 1876 by the law lords, comprising senior judges appointed to fulfil the judicial function of the House as the highest court of appeal (see Chapter 2) and who (from 1887) served for life, but with their membership not passing to their heirs. Two law lords were appointed initially, and the number increased over the years (reaching twelve in 1994). They ceased to be members in 2009, with the creation of the Supreme Court. However, as life peers, the original law lords were early examples of what by the end of the twentieth century was to be the norm.

As a result of Acts passed in 1958 and 1999 (see Chapter 2), the lords temporal have moved from comprising a body of hereditary peers to being one predominantly of life peers, those appointed on individual merit, their titles and place in the House ceasing upon their death.

The creation of peers is a prerogative power – in the gift of the Crown – but is exercised on behalf of the Crown by the Prime Minister. In practice, party leaders nominate members to sit on their party benches (usually after the Prime Minister has decided that new creations should be made); since 2000 an independent appointments commission has nominated the cross-bench peers. (The commission also vets for propriety those nominated by party leaders.) Who they nominate is a matter for the leaders and the independent commission, although the commission has published criteria that it utilises.

It was previously the practice that some prominent figures would receive peerages in recognition of their public service and were not necessarily expected to contribute to the work of the House, but now the expectation is that those who receive peerages will contribute to its work. Peers' contribution to the House is formally unremunerated – there is no salary – but since the 1950s there has been provision for members to claim an attendance allowance.[1]

There is no limit on the number of peers that can be created. At various points in history the membership of the House has been relatively small, but it grew significantly in the twentieth century. There were just over 600 peers at the start of the century, but more than 1,200 by the 1990s. After most hereditary peers were removed by the House of Lords Act 1999 (see below), the number almost halved – to just over 660 – but it grew again in succeeding years. Occasionally, as a result of deaths and resignations, the number has gone down slightly, but the underlying trend has been an upward one: new creations have outnumbered departures. At the start of September 2016, the number was just below 800 (excluding peers on leave of absence and those excluded from membership while they hold particular posts, such as judges), making the House the second-largest second chamber in the world, after the Chinese National People's Congress.

From the early nineteenth century until the passage of the 1999 Act, the House was notable also for being dominated by one party, the Conservatives. Although many peers failed to declare a political affiliation, there was a clear Conservative predominance among the active membership (many peers did not attend), and a notable imbalance when the Labour Party emerged as the principal opposition party in the 1920s. The Conservative dominance, as we shall see, was brought to end by the 1999 Act. Since then, no party has enjoyed a majority in the House of Lords. The size and political composition of the House as of 1 September 2016 are shown in Table 1.2.

Table 1.2 Composition of the House of Lords, 1 September 2016

Conservative	243
Labour	209
Liberal Democrat	105
Crossbench	172
Bishops	26
Non-affiliated	25
Other	16
Total	**796**

Note: Excludes peers on leave of absence and those excluded from membership while they hold particular posts. 'Non-affiliated' comprises peers who hold certain public offices or who have chosen not to join the cross-bench group. 'Other' comprises essentially minor parties such as Democratic Unionist, Plaid Cymru, Green and UKIP.
Source: www.parliament.uk.

Approaches to reform

Identifying what the House of Lords does is necessary for appreciating why it matters to the political system. Looking at who sits in the House is necessary as a prelude to discussing reform of the House. It is notable that demands for reform of the Lords in the twenty-first century have focused not on functions but on composition. Not all critics accept the need for a second chamber, but of those that do there is an acceptance that the tasks fulfilled by the Lords are appropriate to a complementary second chamber. Successive governments, in making the case for introducing some element of election for membership, have confirmed that they wish to retain the existing functions of the House. In 2011 the coalition government published its White Paper (a document outlining government policy) advancing its case for a House with 80 per cent of the members elected. It recorded the existing functions of the House, acknowledged the value of those functions, and declared: 'The Government believes that these functions should remain unchanged when the House of Lords is reformed and that it should continue this valuable work' (HM Government 2011: 10).

Demands for reform focus therefore on what is termed input legitimacy (how members are chosen) rather than on output legitimacy (what it does) (Kelso 2006: 563–81). Debate about the future composition of the House often lacks clarity and sometimes is confused by people talking past one another: proponents of election are countered by the argument that the present House works well. The debate is also frequently mired in claims that are often taken as self-evidently true and therefore not developed.

In order to give shape to the debate, we identify four approaches to reform: the four Rs of *retain* (keep the House as an appointed chamber), *reform* (have a minority of members elected), *replace* (have most or all members elected), and *remove altogether* (abolish the House and have a unicameral Parliament) (Norton 1982: 116–33). The term 'reform' is frequently used generically, but here we employ it is as a distinct approach to change.

The four approaches are mutually exclusive and encompass the different arguments surrounding the future composition of the House. The focus is primarily, though not exclusively, on the composition of the House. It is entirely possible, for example, to make a case to retain an appointed House, but undertake reform of the structures or powers of the House. The retain approach, as we shall see, does indeed encompass proponents who wish to strengthen the existing House in fulfilling its functions and advocate changes to the structures and practices of the House. These changes, though, are essentially internal to the existing House. The essential divide between the first approach and the second and third approaches is one of election. Those in the retain category are opposed to any element of election.

In the following chapter, we look at the origins and development of the House of Lords and the reforms implemented, or proposed, in the period since 1911. In Chapters 3 to 6, we address the current debate, each chapter addressing one of the four Rs. Each adopts the same format, identifying those who support that particular approach and the arguments deployed in its support. We conclude by looking at the future of the United Kingdom's second chamber.

Note

1   By the end of the century, peers could claim attendance allow-ances up to a specified maximum to cover overnight accom-modation, subsistence, and secretarial and research support. These were abolished in 2010 and replaced with a single and exhaustive allowance (excluding travel costs): a peer can claim a flat-rate attendance allowance of either £300 or £150 a day and has to attend the chamber (or committee) in order to qualify to receive it.

2

Achieving change: reforms, 1911 to 2015

THE House of Lords has its origins in the courts of medieval kings, starting with the Anglo-Saxon *Witenagemot* and its Norman successor, the *Curia Regis*. The king summoned his barons – the main landowners – and leading churchmen to court so that they could offer advice and help declare the law. It became the practice that if a baron attended regularly, his heir would be summoned to court following the baron's death. The court thus acquired a hereditary element, barons attending because they had inherited their places rather than in their own right as tenants of the king.

In the thirteenth century, knights from the counties, and later burgesses from various towns, were summoned to court to provide support for the king in raising taxes. The summoning of the knights and burgesses constituted the origins of the House of Commons (McKenzie 1968: 17). Initially, the knights and burgesses met with the barons and churchmen – at least, on those occasions when a court was summoned – but in the fourteenth century the knights and burgesses started to meet separately from the barons and churchmen, thus creating what became the two chambers of the House of Commons and the House of Lords. The country acquired a bicameral legislature.

Parliament was summoned only when the king needed support – there were some lengthy periods when it was never called – and ultimate power rested with the monarch. However, within the first two centuries of its existence, Parliament developed functions that rendered it a significant political body. The king became dependent on Parliament's assent to raising money through taxation, and Parliament began to insist on grievances being redressed before it gave such assent. People could petition Parliament, and from the use of petitions developed the practice of declaring law through statutes – approved by Lords, Commons, and King – as distinct from ordinances, which were promulgated solely by the king. Statute law soon became more prolific than ordinances and the task of writing statutes passed from the king's scribes to the House of Commons.

Parliament also maintained a judicial function. Justice was administered by the king and his court in Parliament, but in the fifteenth century it was held that the judicial authority of the high court of Parliament lay not with Parliament as a whole, but with the House of Lords.[1]

The Commons became more significant under Tudor monarchs, who sought support for taxation and in the religious battles that characterised the sixteenth century. Within Parliament, both Houses were for most purposes co-equal, but in matters of money the Commons asserted the right to initiate taxation. The Lords became more significant under the early Stuarts and served something of a mediating role between king and Commons (Perceval 1954: 39). However, attempts at mediation proved ultimately unsuccessful in the face of Stuart assertions of the divine right of kings (that their power derived from God rather than Parliament or the people), resulting under Charles I in a civil war and a break in the continuity of the House of Lords. Most peers sided with the king. In 1649 the House of Commons asserted its authority over the king and the House of Lords and declared that the people were, under God, the origin of all just power and that the Commons, being chosen by the people, held the supreme power of the nation. 'The House of Lords was not automatically abolished, but their *raison d'etre* was removed. Abolition was to follow on 19 March' (Longford 1988: 77). A second chamber, 'the Other House', was summoned in 1658–59, but the Parliament was soon dissolved and that proved to be the end of the 'Other House'.

The House of Lords came back into being as a result of the Restoration of 1660 (a deliberate attempt was made to restore what had preceded the demise of the monarch) and the House was soon to be an important political actor. Various lords played a central role in the transfer of power from James II – who fled the country in 1688 – to Mary (James's daughter) and her husband, William of Orange. William and Mary accepted the Bill of Rights of 1689, which established the supremacy of Parliament – the monarch could no longer legislate without the assent of Parliament. Parliament still looked to the monarch to take the lead, but it was no longer possible to rule without Parliament.

The House of Lords was a significant force in the eighteenth century, not least during the reign of Queen Anne, and continued as a co-equal part of Parliament. Although the Commons continued to assert its privilege in matters of finance – denying the right of the Lords to amend bills raising money – the two Houses were otherwise equals. Indeed, the House of Lords was important not only as one of the two chambers of the legislature but also because of who sat in it. Peers were typically powerful landowners and could control who were returned as MPs in their area; many constituencies were 'pocket boroughs', essentially in the gift of those who owned the land. A table compiled about 1815 showed that 471 seats were controlled by 144 peers and 123 commoners (Ostrogorski 1902: 20). Some peers exerted their influence as much through the House of Commons as the House of Lords. Some were powerful political figures in their own right, being appointed as ministers or, on occasion, as Prime Minister. There were some notably aristocratic Cabinets well into the nineteenth century.

However, the power of the House of Lords began to be challenged in the nineteenth century. Pressure for a political voice from a burgeoning middle class and a growing body of artisans led to political reform, especially in the form of an extension of the franchise and reform of constituency boundaries. The Representation of the People Acts (the Reform Acts) of 1832, 1867, and 1884 transformed the political landscape of Britain. They resulted in a House of Commons that had some claim to be a representative chamber – after 1884, a majority of working men had the vote – and prompted the growth of mass-membership political parties, parties that fought general elections to win a majority of seats in the House of Commons.

Although the House of Lords continued to assert its position as co-equal with the Commons, some peers recognised the implications of the changes. Speaking during debate on the 1867 Reform Bill, the Earl of Shaftesbury queried how the House would be affected by 'this great democratic change':

> So long as the other House of Parliament was elected upon a restricted principle, I can understand that it would submit to a check from a House such as this. But in the presence of this great democratic power and the advance of this great democratic wave ... it passes my comprehension to understand how an hereditary House like this can hold its own. It might be possible for this House, in one instance, to withstand a measure if it were violent, unjust, and coercive; but I do not believe that the repetition of such an offence would be permitted. It would be said, 'The people must govern, and not a set of hereditary peers never chosen by the people'. (*Parliamentary Debates*, Vol. 188, cols 1925–6, cited Norton 1981: 21)

In the event, peers sought to maintain their capacity to determine the fate of legislation by arguing that they should exercise their power if the opinion of the nation was unclear, and force an election to determine that opinion (Norton 2013: 156–7; Weston 1986: 461–88). Not only was the House unelected; it also had (from the beginning of the nineteenth century) a Conservative majority. As the Liberal MP Sir Charles Dilke observed, this was essentially a recipe for annual parliaments when the Liberals were in office, and septennial parliaments when the Conservatives were in office (Norton 1981: 22). In 1884 the House refused to pass the Liberal government's franchise bill until a scheme of redistribution of seats was introduced. In 1893 it voted down a Home Rule Bill for Ireland. The Liberals adopted a policy of 'mend or end', and in 1894 the Liberal Party conference voted to abolish the Lords' veto. A period of Conservative government then followed, and the century ended with no changes to the powers of the House.

Reforming the powers, 1911–49

The situation changed following the return of a Liberal government in 1906. The Lords amended or forced the abandonment of a number of bills, and in 1909 the House rejected the budget. The rejection triggered a general election, held at the start of 1910. The Liberal government lost seats, but had a majority sufficient to pass the budget, which was now accepted by the Lords. However, the government then pursued a bill to limit the powers of the House of Lords. It was resisted in the Lords, but after a second general election, and the indication from the king that he was willing to create sufficient new peers to pass the bill, the bill was accepted by the Lords (Norton 2013: 155–69). The Parliament Act 1911 defined the relationship between the two Houses, confirming in statute the supremacy of the elected House.

Under the 1911 Act, a money bill (one dealing wholly with money, and certified as such by the Speaker) becomes law one month after leaving the Commons, whether approved by the Lords or not. Non-money bills could be delayed by the Lords for two successive sessions, but if passed in identical form by the Commons in the third session the bill was to become law. The only exceptions were bills starting their life in the Lords, bills to extend the life of a Parliament, and delegated legislation. The Act also reduced the maximum life of a Parliament from seven years to five.

The provisions of the Act were used to pass two measures: the Welsh Church Act 1914 and the Government of Ireland Act 1914. However, no further recourse was had to its provisions for the next thirty years. After the return of a Labour government with a large majority in 1945, the Conservative leader in the Lords, Viscount Cranborne (later Marquess of Salisbury), enunciated what became known as the Salisbury doctrine – that the Lords would not reject measures promised in a government's election manifesto. Although the House followed this doctrine and the Labour government under Clement Attlee achieved its reforming legislation, ministers were worried in case peers should use their powers towards the end of the Parliament to frustrate the will of the government. (They were particularly concerned about their legislation to nationalise the coal and steel industries.) As a result, the government introduced a bill to reduce the delaying power of the Lords from two sessions to one. The measure reached the statute book as the Parliament Act 1949, under the provisions of the 1911 Act.

The Parliament Acts deal exclusively with powers. Neither the Liberal government of 1906 nor the Labour government of 1945 attempted to deal with composition. In the controversy following the rejection of the 1909 budget, it was Conservative peers who argued for a reform of composition: they preferred that to limiting the powers of the House.

Reforming composition 1958–2015

The latter half of the twentieth century witnessed various changes to the composition of the House, but of those enacted, none introduced an elected element. One government reform measure failed to make it to the statute book, but again that entailed no element of election. Only in the twenty-first century have successive governments advanced policies for a partly elected or predominantly elected House, culminating in 2012 in a bill to provide for a House with 80 per cent of the members elected. In the event, as we shall see, that failed to make it to the statute book.

The twentieth century saw three government measures reach the statute book that changed the composition of the House, and one that failed. The three that were enacted were the Life Peerages Act 1958, the Peerage Act 1963, and the House of Lords Act 1999. The measure that failed to be enacted was the Parliament (No. 2) Bill in 1969.

The Life Peerages Act 1958 effected a seminal change in the nature of the House of Lords. The House was by the 1950s a largely moribund chamber. It had declined from the heady days of the nineteenth century and early years of the twentieth. Many hereditary peers were busy elsewhere and rarely attended. Bromhead estimated in 1957 that, out of 860 members, there were 'some sixty peers who may be regarded as a nucleus of regular attenders' (Bromhead 1958: 31). Often the House met for only three days a week, and a sitting might last no more than three hours. It attracted little attention and was not contributing notably to the political process. As a means of strengthening the House and giving it some greater legitimacy, the Conservative government of Harold Macmillan introduced a bill to enable members to be appointed for life. This meant that some who were opposed to the hereditary principle could be made peers on merit and without their titles – and membership of the Lords – passing to their heirs. It also provided for women to be appointed to the House. The 1958 Act led to people from a range of backgrounds being appointed as life peers. Their number included some distinguished women – styled women peers on their own insistence, to distinguish them from peeresses, that is, those who had inherited their titles or were the wives of hereditary peers.

The effect of life peerages was to create a more active House. Life peers were disproportionately active and, as their number grew, so did the activity of the House. The House sat for longer, became more specialised, and members displayed somewhat greater independence in their behaviour than before (Baldwin 1985, Grantham and Moore Hodgson 1985). Life peerages were conferred on a range of people who had reached eminence in various fields – the law, science, trade unions, education, medicine, and the arts, among others. The House was able to become more specialised through the use of committees, not least in the scrutiny of European legislation. The House, in effect, began to reinvent itself, not least as an effective complementary chamber fulfilling the functions detailed in Chapter 1.

The Peerage Act 1963 was concerned with members leaving the House rather than joining it. On the face of it, the measure was a modest one, enabling hereditary peers to renounce their titles. Few were to do so, but some who did were politically high-profile figures. The Act was the consequence of a campaign led by the second Viscount Stansgate – Anthony Wedgwood Benn (later better known simply as Tony Benn) – who had no wish to leave the Commons and join the Lords when his father died, but who under the law had no option. The 1963 Act enabled him to renounce his title and seek re-election to the Commons. The Act had another politically significant consequence: it allowed the then Foreign Secretary, the Earl of Home, to be chosen as Prime Minister. Upon appointment, he renounced his title and successfully sought election to the Commons in a by-election. Had the measure not been passed, he would have been prevented from becoming Prime Minister by virtue of the convention that the premier must sit in the elected House. The Act remains on the statute book, but has largely been rendered redundant by the passage of the House of Lords Act 1999.

The next attempt at reform came later in the 1960s, under the Labour government of Harold Wilson. The Parliament (No. 2) Bill, which came before the Commons in 1969 was designed primarily to remove the voting power of hereditary peers. Under the bill, existing hereditary peers (other than those of first creation) would be non-voting members, and those inheriting their titles after enactment of the measure would no longer be members by virtue of that inheritance.

The bill was not seen as a notably radical measure, and it elicited no great enthusiasm, even on the part of government. As the Prime Minister, Harold Wilson, recorded: 'In moving the second reading, I made no effort to suggest that there was any enthusiasm about the Bill, one way or another' (Wilson 1971: 608). In the event, any enthusiasm came from opponents, led on the Labour benches by Michael Foot, who felt that the bill was not radical enough (he favoured abolition), and on the Conservative benches by Enoch Powell, who felt that it went too far (he supported the status quo). They led a spirited group of opponents, while supporters lacked sufficient will to stay late hours to get the bill through, and it was eventually withdrawn (Morgan 1975: 213–18).

The issue of Lords reform was returned to by the Labour government of Tony Blair, elected in 1997. It had a manifesto commitment to remove hereditary peers from the Lords and it achieved passage of the House of Lords Act 1999 to give effect to that commitment. At the beginning of 1999 there were over 1,200 members of the Lords, approximately two-thirds of them hereditary peers. Under a deal done to facilitate passage of the bill, ninety-two hereditary peers were retained. The rest ceased to be members. As we have seen (Chapter 1), following passage of the Act there were just over 660 members remaining in the House. Of these, all bar the ninety-two hereditary peers and twenty-six lords spiritual were life peers.

Combined with the 1958 Life Peerages Act, the 1999 Act completed a transformation of the second chamber. It was no longer a body composed primarily of members who sat by inheritance (many of whom were notable by their absence) and who mostly supported the Conservative cause. Aristocracy gave way to a form of meritocracy, members being appointed on their individual merit to contribute to the work of the House. The Conservative dominance gave way to a House in which no one party enjoyed a majority.

The House after 1999 was notable for being more active in terms of daily attendance – especially expressed as a proportion of the membership – and for being more willing to challenge government. Peers saw themselves as having greater legitimacy to call government to account and, if necessary, to defeat it in the division lobbies. As we have seen (Chapter 1), ministers have therefore had to take the House seriously and to engage with members.

Two other measures have made it to the statute book in the twenty-first century, both of them private members' bills. The House of Lords Reform Act 2014, sponsored by Conservative MP Dan Byles and taken up in the Lords by Liberal Democrat Lord Steel, allowed peers to retire. (Life peers cannot renounce their titles and, until this Act, could not formally cease to be members of the House.) It also provided for the expulsion of peers who commit serious criminal offences and removes those who fail to attend for a whole session. The House of Lords (Expulsion and Suspension) Act 2015, sponsored by cross-bench peer Baroness Hayman (a former Lord Speaker) and taken up in the Commons by Conservative MP Sir George Young, gave the House the power to expel members, something not previously possible, and also extended its power to suspend members. Both measures emanated from a cross-party group, the Campaign for an Effective Second Chamber (see Chapter 3), and were not opposed by government.

The result of these measures has been to strengthen the House of Lords as a body in fulfilling its core functions. As we have noted, its work in carrying them out has not been the source of major criticism. Where critics see the measures as not going far enough is in the retention, under the 1999 Act, of ninety-two hereditary peers – and the fact that when one of them dies, another is elected (either by other hereditary peers in the House or by the whole House) to replace them – and in the more pervasive failure to provide for an element of popular election.

The failure to reform – the House of Lords Reform Bill 2012

The passage of the House of Lords Act 1999 constituted, for the Labour government of Tony Blair, stage 1 of Lords reform. The government appointed a royal commission to recommend what further reforms should take place (stage 2). The commission (the Wakeham Commission) recommended a partly elected House and the government embraced this approach. However, its stance received little political support and no bill was ever introduced. Instead, a joint committee was appointed to consider reform: it identified a range of options and in 2003 each House was invited to vote on them. MPs voted against *all* the options (all appointed, partly elected, largely or wholly elected) as well as against an amendment for a unicameral legislature. The Lords voted overwhelmingly for a wholly appointed House and against all the other options. Perhaps not surprisingly, given the outcome in the Commons, the government took no action on the issue. In 2007, MPs and peers were invited to vote again on the various options. The Lords maintained their position and voted for a wholly appointed House (and against all the other options), but in the Commons there was a majority for an 80 per cent elected and a 100 per cent elected House. In the light of how MPs had voted, the government decided to adopt a policy of having a largely elected House. Its White Paper, *The Governance of Britain* (HM Government 2007), said that it was committed to enacting the will of the House of Commons, but plans for a draft bill, announced in February 2010, were overtaken by the calling of a general election.

Instead, the next attempt at legislative reform took place under the coalition government formed in 2010. Both parties to the coalition had manifesto commitments to support a predominantly elected House of Lords. For the Liberal Democrats this was one of two most important constitutional reforms they wished to achieve (the other was a new electoral system for parliamentary elections). As part of the negotiations to form a coalition, it was agreed to set up a committee to produce a draft bill 'to bring forward proposals for a wholly or mainly elected upper chamber on the basis of proportional representation'. In 2011, the government published a draft bill providing for a House of just over 300 members, with 240 elected and 60 appointed members, plus twelve bishops, the elected members to be returned under the single transferable vote (STV). Elections were to take place at the same time as elections to the House of Commons. Members would serve for a non-renewable fixed term of three election cycles (expected to be fifteen years). The bill was sent to a joint committee for pre-legislative scrutiny. The joint committee recommended that the proposed change be subject to a referendum. Almost half the members also published an 'alternative report' arguing for the issue to be addressed by a convention looking at constitutional change as a whole and not treating this as a discrete issue.

The government rejected the proposal for a referendum and introduced its House of Lords Reform Bill in 2012. It followed the main provisions of the draft bill, the main difference being the inclusion of a regional list system of election in place of STV. The bill attracted considerable criticism from Conservative MPs – some organised themselves into a group known as 'the sensibles' and lobbied hard against it (Norton 2015: 481). Some MPs opposed it on principle: they were opposed to an elected chamber that could challenge the primacy of the Commons. Others were opposed to the detail of the bill, objecting not least to non-renewable fixed terms (removing any element of account-ability). One MP who supported an elected second chamber told this writer that he was opposed to the measure. 'Why?' 'I have read the bill!' During the two-day debate on second reading on 9 and 10 July, opponents on the Conservative benches dominated. When the motion for second reading was put, it was passed by a large majority – 462 votes to 124 – but the 'no' lobby included ninety-one Conservatives; a further nineteen abstained. It was the largest rebellion by government MPs on the second reading of a bill in post-war history. This signalled problems for the Conservative part of the coalition. However, the fate of the bill was sealed by what happened next.

The Labour Opposition had supported the principle of the bill and therefore voted for second reading. However, it felt that more time was needed for discussing the bill than was provided in the government's programme motion. It therefore made clear that it would vote against the motion. Conservative MPs opposed to the bill were also going to vote against. This meant that there would be enough votes to defeat it, and in the light of this, the government did not move the motion. The effect was to kill the bill. Without a formal timetable for the bill, opponents would do what Michael Foot and Enoch Powell and their allies had done in 1969 – talk endlessly, and in effect filibuster, denying the government the opportunity to make progress on other business. (Because it was a bill of constitutional significance, committee stage would have been taken on the floor of the House.) Recognis-ing the inevitable, the following month the Deputy Prime Minister, Nick Clegg, announced that the government would not proceed with the bill.

The fate of the 2012 bill meant that reform of the Lords was off the government's agenda for the rest of the Parliament and, in the eyes of many politicians, for the foreseeable future.

It is noteworthy that what change has been achieved to the Lords in the twenty-first century has been primarily the result of backbench initiative and that government attempts at reform – in 2012, as in 1969 – have failed not in the House of Lords but in the House of Commons. Ministers have tended to anticipate opposition from peers, but have been unable to mobilise sufficient support on the benches behind them in the Commons in order to get their bills onto the statute book. For some MPs, the attempts at changing the composition of the House of Lords are either steps too far or not bold enough.

Note

1   Few peers had legal qualifications and the House did not develop as a major court, exercising primarily appellate jurisdiction, until the eighteenth century. By the mid-nineteenth century the convention had developed that peers who were not legally qualified did not participate in judicial proceedings. Cases after 1948 were heard not in the chamber but in an appellate committee. In essence, the judicial work of the House was carried out essentially independently of the deliberative work of the House as a legislative chamber.

3

Retain

THE core defining argument of the retain approach is that the House of Lords should remain an appointed chamber. Any element of election is opposed.

Retain can be divided between those who see no need for change at all and those who accept some need to change both the structures and the composition of the House, but without the need for an elected element. Those falling into the former category include MPs such as the late Enoch Powell, who led opposition to the Parliament (No. 2) Bill in 1969. For him, the composition of the House was the result of prescription and should not be subject to artificial change. The House of Lords, he argued, 'is an integral part of Parliament simply because that is how Parliament evolved, and its powers, like those of the House of Commons, derive not from theory, but from precedent' (quoted in Forsyth 2012: 72). Those falling into the latter category include the Labour government of 1966–70, which introduced the Parliament (No. 2) Bill, and the Blair government in its first two years of office, both of which sought to remove all or most hereditary peers from the House.

Also falling in the latter category is the Campaign for an Effective Second Chamber, a cross-party group of peers and MPs opposed to an elected chamber but supporting change to enhance the existing chamber. Created in 2001, it has made much of the running in arguing for incremental change and has the distinction of having achieved more legislative change than the government in the 2010–15 Parliament. It was responsible for initiating the two private members' bills that made it onto the statute book – the House of Lords Reform Act 2014 and the House of Lords (Expulsion and Suspension) Act 2015. It advocates further change, including limiting the size of the House, imposing more rigorous criteria of merit for appointment to the House, and removing the provision for the remaining hereditary peers to be replaced when one of them dies or retires. The emphasis is on strengthening the existing House and defending what the group regards as its strengths as a value-adding chamber.

We are concerned here with the arguments advanced by those who have a principled belief in retaining an appointed second chamber, as distinct from governments which have ended up maintaining the existing House essentially as a default option or because they have not mobilised sufficient support to achieve a measure of election.

The principled case for the appointed chamber is essentially twofold. First, appointment facilitates the recruitment of people who are particularly well suited to fulfilling the functions of the House. Second, having an appointed chamber is justifiable on democratic grounds. Appointment ensures that the accountability of government to electors through the first chamber is not compromised.

Those advocating an appointed House stress that form should follow function. For them, appointment is the most appropriate means of ensuring effective delivery of the generally agreed functions of the House. The House of Lords can be characterised as a house of experience and expertise, the Life Peerages Act having transformed the nature of the membership (Baldwin 1993: 56). It is common for people to be appointed as peers because of their experience, for example, having served in posts such as a senior Cabinet minister, chief of the defence staff, general-secretary of the Trades Union Congress, Lord Chief Justice, or head of a charity. They are complemented by others who are appointed because of their individual achievements, such as leading figures in sport (such as Paralympian Tanni Grey-Thompson) or campaigners such as Doreen Lawrence, mother of murdered teenager Stephen Lawrence, and John Bird, founder of *The Big Issue* magazine.

Some are appointed because they are the leading experts in their field – that is, they are highly trained and have reached the top of their profession. The House includes leading lawyers, doctors, scientists, and academics. Although some of those who have served in public positions are ennobled once they have finished their service, it is not unusual for experts to be appointed whose expertise is current – that is, they continue to serve in their professional role. They can thus contribute to debates on the basis of existing knowledge in their field, rather than knowledge of the position some years earlier.

The benefit of appointing such people to the House is that they can subject bills and government actions to informed scrutiny in a way that is not possible in the House of Commons. The House of Commons has become dominated by career politicians (those who, in Max Weber's terms, 'live for politics') who seek election as MPs at a young age and devote themselves to a political career (King 1981, Riddell 1993, 1995). They may be very able, both intellectually and politically, but they have not built up a career in a particular non-political field; they may specialise in a subject, such as health, but they are not experts (that is, trained and qualified in the subject). This places even greater stress on the value of the Lords as a complementary chamber. Peers can look at measures from a different perspective to MPs and engage with ministers on the basis of an informed knowledge of the subject, often superior to that of the ministers taking a measure through the House.

Furthermore, and this is what establishes the unique value of the House, it provides an arena for a discourse of civil society. This was a point made by the Chief Rabbi, Lord Sacks, in his evidence to the joint committee on the draft House of Lords Reform Bill (Sacks 2012: 175–8). There is a discourse not just with government, but between the parts of civil society from which members of the House are drawn. That sets the House apart, generating value that would be lost in an elected House or if experts were available only to advise parliamentary committees.

On this argument, it is not clear what value would be added by replacing the experience and expertise of peers with elected members who would not be that distinguishable from members of the House of Commons. The assumption – not confined to those who support an appointed House – is that those who would seek election to the second chamber would be politicians who would prefer to be elected to the first chamber, but have failed to achieve that goal. This appears to be conceded by governments in making the case for election: government white papers advocating some element of election have proposed that a person having served in an elected second chamber should be barred for some years from seeking election to the House of Commons.

Election would also squeeze out the independent element of the House. It is a rare for an Independent MP to be elected. In the Lords, as we have seen, over 20 per cent of members are cross-bench peers. Survey data, as we shall see (Table 3.1), show that the public do not necessarily accord high importance to having a large number of independent members. However, the public do accord importance to having members who are experts in their field, and a good number of experts are to be found on the cross-benches. By their nature, experts are often non-partisan.

Appointment not only enables independent members to serve in the House, but is also a means of ensuring that members are drawn from a wide range of backgrounds. Party selection committees may demonstrate particular preferences in selecting candidates for parliamentary elections: the preference historically has tended to be for white, male, middle-class (and, in the past, Anglican, and married) candidates. Although the situation has changed, there remain problems. Appointment to the Lords enables people who are disadvantaged by the biases in such a procedure to be given a voice in the parliamentary process. There are more members in the Lords than in the Commons drawn from black and minority ethnic backgrounds. The first black woman member of the Cabinet was a peer (Baroness Amos), as was the first Muslim member of the Cabinet (Baroness Warsi). The House also has more disabled (not least, wheelchair-bound, as well as blind) members than the Commons. Although women comprise fewer than 25 per cent of the membership, their number and

Table 3.1   Public views of which factors are important to determining Lords' legitimacy, in rank order

	Important			
	Very	Fairly	Not very	Not at all
Trust in the appointments process	76%	19%	3%	2%
That the House considers legislation carefully	73%	23%	3%	1%
That many members are experts in their field	54%	36%	8%	2%
That the House acts in accordance with public opinion	53%	32%	11%	4%
That there are some members elected by the public	50%	34%	12%	4%
A fair balance of seats between the parties	46%	41%	9%	3%
Presence of numerous independent members	41%	42%	13%	4%

Note: 'Don't knows' excluded from calculations.
Source: Russell 2007: 4.

proportion have grown in recent decades, not least through the nominations of the independent appointments commission. (It is notable also that women are prominent in leadership positions in the House.) The House (like the House of Commons) is far from being a microcosm of society, but the appointment process, and the turnover of members through either death or, now, retirement, means that changes can be made more speedily than is the case with selection of candidates for the elected House.

Supporters of an appointed chamber argue, then, that it is fit for purpose in terms of fulfilling what is expected of it. They contend that is also in line with public expectations. If people are given a binary choice between an elected and an appointed chamber, they opt for the former. However, if other options are factored in, including the functions of the House, they tend to accord greater importance to fulfilling the functions of the House than to having an elected element. This was demonstrated by an Ipsos MORI poll carried out in 2007 (Table 3.1). It found that in determining the legitimacy of the House of Lords, factors such as its considering legislation carefully and in detail and having many members who are experts in the field were notably ahead of having some members elected by the public.

There is also survey evidence that the public think that the House of Lords carries out its work effectively. An ICM poll for the think-tank Politeia in 2005 found that 72 per cent of respondents thought that the House of Lords did a very or fairly good job; only 23 per cent thought that it did a fairly or very bad job. In the same poll, 71 per cent thought that the House provided an effective check on the power of government.

Supporters of retaining an appointed House thus stress the output legitimacy of the House (what it does). However, they also take on critics who challenge the House in terms of input legitimacy (how it is chosen). The argument that an appointed chamber is inherently 'undemocratic' – a charge levelled as if it is self-evidently true – is contested. An appointed second chamber is consistent with having a democratic political system.

Democracy is usually defined, based on its roots – *demos* (people) and *kratos* (rule) – as 'rule of or by the people'. In other words, it is about how people govern themselves. Given the sheer size of the population in a nation, representative democracy is substituted for direct democracy. Fundamental to a representative democracy is the ability of the people to choose who will govern on their behalf and then to hold those in government to account for their actions. In the UK, government is chosen through elections to the House of Commons. People vote for the party that they wish to form a government. Parties seek election on a particular programme and, if elected to government, seek to implement that programme. If electors believe that the government has failed to deliver what they expect of it, they can hold it to account by removing it from office at the next general election. Election day is, in the words of philosopher Karl Popper, 'judgement day'. Electors know who is responsible for public policy – the party (or parties) in government – and can act to reward or punish that body. There is no divided responsibility. The government cannot hive off responsibility for public policy. There is what may be termed core accountability (Norton 2011a). The House of Lords adds value to the political process by fulfilling functions that complement the elected chamber, but does not challenge the ability of government, through the House of Commons, to get its way. Conflict between the two has been the exception and not the norm. On only four occasions since the passage of the Parliament Act 1949 has an Act been passed under the provisions of the Parliament Acts.

Election of the second chamber would, it is argued, threaten that accountability at the heart of the political system. An elected House might not claim to be co-equal with the Commons – elected second chambers typically do not enjoy the same powers as first chambers – but it is likely that it would demand more powers and/or employ the existing powers in a way that the current House does not. Rather than focus on the detail, members might challenge the ends of a bill and decline to pass it. There would be no grounds, for example, for maintaining the Salisbury convention. Given that it is a convention, members would be within their rights to ignore it.

Even though the Parliament Acts could be used to ensure the outcome wanted by the Commons, the second chamber could still cause enormous difficulties, especially towards the end of a Parliament. Members might also challenge the premise of the Parliament Acts and seek a new settlement between the two Houses. Supporters of election variously cite the preamble to the Parliament Act 1911, which stated that 'it is intended to substitute for the House of Lords as it presently exists a Second Chamber constituted on a popular instead of a hereditary basis'.

However, it then went on to say that any such measure would need to define the powers of the House. There was a recognition, or at least what Rowland termed a hint, that 'the powers of a reconstituted Upper House would be greater than those which the Bill would leave to the House of Lords' (Rowland 1968: 297; see also Jenkins 1954: 136).

An elected House might thus claim an electoral mandate to challenge the first chamber and, if it did so, might conflict with MPs and demand outcomes that would differ from those promised to electors by the party successful in being returned to government. Deals done between the two Houses might favour not electors but (as in the USA) special interests. In the USA, there is notable public dissatisfaction with interest-group influence and the processes of Congress (Hibbing and Theiss-Morse 1995). The principal problem, then, is whom do electors hold to account for the outcomes of public policy? An elected second chamber would hold out the prospect of divided accountability, with no obvious benefit to electors. As Professor Colin Tyler, a specialist in democratic theory, has put it:

> democratising one part of Parliament (the Lords) will reduce the democratic character of the whole (Parliament). And ultimately it is the democratic character of Parliament that matters, not the democratic character of its constituent parts considered in isolation from each other. (Tyler 2012: 200)

Supporters of appointment thus stress the value of the existing composition against the prospect of divided accountability and the loss of expertise and independence, with no obvious benefit delivered by what could be a duplicate of the House of Commons. If the second chamber ended up as a mirror image of the Commons, it would be superfluous. If it ended up with a different political composition and kept challenging the Commons, it would undermine the accountability at the heart of the political system. If it were partly elected, it would be unstable, Labour MP David Clelland arguing in 2007 that it would 'lead to a conflict with some Members claiming legitimacy and others not' (*House of Commons Debates*, 7 March 2007, col. 1553).

There is the additional problem that in the United Kingdom – a unitary state – it is not clear on what basis electors would be casting their ballots for members of the second chamber. In a federal state, second chambers can represent the states of the nation – electors vote as citizens of their state; they vote as citizens of the nation for members of the first chamber. In the UK, electors would be voting on the same basis for members of the second chamber as for the first.

Supporters of an appointed House also draw on survey data to show that electors accord no priority to the issue, even if they favour some measure of election. Successive polls have shown that members of the public think that there are more important things for government to do. An Ipsos MORI poll in July 2012 found that almost three-quarters of those questioned (72 per cent) believed the government should be focusing on other issues.

Survey data have also revealed that electors hold conflicting views. A Populus poll in 2006 found that 72 per cent of respondents believed that 'at least half of the members of the House of Lords should be elected so that the upper chamber of Parliament has democratic legitimacy'. The very same poll found that 75 per cent thought that 'The House of Lords should remain a mainly appointed house because this gives it a degree of independence from electoral politics and allows people with a broad range of experience and expertise to be involved in the law-making process.' Supporters of the existing House thus have grounds for claiming some public recognition of the work of the House and a desire not to lose the attributes that enable it to fulfil its work effectively.

Those wishing to retain the existing House also raise the issue of cost. Having an appointed House, it is argued, saves public money. There are two dimensions to this. One is simply in terms of running costs: the House is efficient and costs far less than the elected House. With no salaries and no provision of staff for individual peers – everything, apart from travel, has to be covered by the attendance allowance – the running costs of the House are notably less than those of the Commons. The cost to the public purse of an MP is approximately four to six times the cost of a peer. The House thus delivers what supporters contend is value for money in a way that an elected chamber, replete with salaries and staff for its members, could not. One peer, former economics editor Lord Lipsey, has estimated that the cost of an elected chamber could be an additional £484 million over five years (*BBC News*, 22 June 2012). The cost argument is incidental to the argument of principle, but it is not insignificant if it means greater cost for less value.

The second dimension is more substantial in terms of the potential compromises that would result from having two elected chambers. Drawing on public choice theory, Stephen MacLean has argued that having two elected chambers would increase the risk of government failure. Elected representatives respond to demands for more expensive programmes, leading to higher levels of taxation or government borrowing (MacLean 2011). There is value in having a House that is independent of such pressures.

In summary, then, the case for retaining an appointed House is justified on empirical and philosophical grounds. It can be justified in terms both of what it does and of how its members are selected; indeed, the latter is a prerequisite for the former. Many of the criticisms levelled at the existing House (be it the extent of prime ministerial patronage or the size of the House) are not arguments for election but, rather, for changes to existing rules and practices. Many retainers, as we have noted, support change within the House to render it an even more effective House. In so doing, they are following the dictum of Edmund Burke that a state without the means of some change is without the means of its own conservation. It is change in order to strengthen and not destroy. For retainers, a wholly appointed House delivers benefits to the political system, and on a scale that alternative systems cannot. For them, the argument for retention is both principled and compelling.

4

Reform

THE case for having some – but not a majority of – members elected, either directly or indirectly, has been made by various bodies. A minority report to the Royal Commission on the Constitution in 1973 recommended that 150 members be added, drawn from the Scottish, Welsh, and Northern Irish assemblies that the commission proposed (Royal Commission on the Constitution 1973: paras. 297–307). However, the most prominent advocacy in recent decades has emanated from the Royal Commission on the Reform of the House of Lords, set up by the Blair government in 1999 and chaired by Conservative peer and former Leader of the House of Lords, Lord Wakeham.

The Wakeham Commission report, *A House for the Future* (Royal Commission on the Reform of the House of Lords 2000), recommended a House of 550 members, with a minority of members elected from the different parts of the UK. It advanced three options for the number to be elected – 65, 87 or 195. It erred towards favouring the second option, with eighty-seven members being elected at the time of each European Parliament (EP) election. The government was sympathetic to the report's recommendations. Indeed, in a 1998 White Paper it had identified the benefits of a part-elected, part-appointed chamber. It responded to the Royal Commission report with a White Paper, *The House of Lords: Completing the Reform* (HM Government 2001), recommending that 20 per cent of the members be elected.

The case for injecting some elected members is that it would, in the words of the Wakeham Commission, remedy some of the defects of the old House of Lords, 'which lacked the political legitimacy and confidence to do its job properly, while preserving some of its best features' (Royal Commission on the Reform of the House of Lords 2000). In other words, it is designed to inject some element of legitimacy deriving from election (input legitimacy) while retaining the existing capacity of the House to fulfil the functions expected of it (output legitimacy). The emphasis is essentially on the latter.

The commission recognised the importance of the functions of the second chamber and also said that it was an error to suppose that the chamber's authority could stem only from democratic election. It favoured having members who were not professional politicians, had experience in a range of different walks of life, and had the knowledge and skills necessary for the House to discharge effectively its roles in relation to human rights and constitutional affairs. The reformed second chamber, it said, 'should continue to include people who can help it to maintain a philosophical, moral and spiritual perspective on public policy issues' (Royal Commission on the Reform of the House of Lords 2000: 101). It recommended against a wholly elected chamber: 'Putting it bluntly but accurately, a wholly elected second chamber would in practice mean that British public life was dominated even more than it is already by professional politicians' (Royal Commission on the Reform of the House of Lords 2000: 106). Total reliance on election, it continued, would in practice be incompatible with ensuring that members had relevant experience and expertise. Nor, it noted, did most electoral systems ensure gender balance or appropriate representation for ethnic, religious, or other minorities.

However, it felt that an elected element would be valuable for providing a direct voice for the various nations and regions of the United Kingdom. Under the first of its three models, sixty-five regional members would be chosen by a system of 'complementary election', based on each party's share of the votes in each region. Under the second model, eighty-seven regional members would be elected at each EP election, employing a similar electoral system as for EP elections. Under the third model, 195 members would be elected using the same system.

Its proposals, it argued, would, by combining an element of election with changes to the appointments process, be more democratic than the existing arrangements, with regional members reflecting the balance of opinion within the regions, as well as more representative, with more gender, ethnic minority, and religious balance. Election would help to achieve the former, and changes to the appointments system would help to achieve the latter.

The government, in its response, *The House of Lords: Completing the Reform* (HM Government 2001), essentially endorsed the recommendations and rationale of the Royal Commission. It wanted to retain an independent element in the House, with a membership distinctive from that of the Commons. It too felt that partial election would provide for a more representative House, but one that would not challenge the primacy of the House of Commons:

> In the case of the UK, where the legitimacy of national Government depends wholly upon elections to, and the support of, the House of Commons, the second chamber does not legitimise Government itself. Its role, rather, is one of a subordinate revising and deliberative chamber, for which direct election has a role to play but is neither a necessary nor a sufficient basis for its membership. (HM Government 2001: 18)

If the second chamber were to be elected, there would be competing authorities. Arguments would, it said, arise on the issue of which chamber had the superior democratic legitimacy based on which electoral system was thought superior. 'Two wholly directly elected chambers within the Westminster system would be a recipe for gridlock and the Government therefore joins the Royal Commission in rejecting this option' (HM Government 2001: 18). It also went on to reject a largely elected chamber on the grounds that it would squeeze out independent members as well as members who have experience and expertise as leaders in different fields. Furthermore, the larger the elected element, the greater the competition to MPs in their representative role.

The election of some, but not a majority of members, would enable the primacy of the House of Commons to be maintained, and allow the House of Lords to continue to fulfil its present functions. With only a minority of members elected, life peers would not feel intimidated by their presence. Election, however, would inject greater legitimacy, or at least a different kind of legitimacy, and enable people in the different parts of the United Kingdom to feel that they had someone to speak for their particular part of the nation in parliamentary debates.

The government favoured a larger House than that proposed by the Royal Commission. It proposed a House of 600 members, which meant that 120 members would be directly elected. Combined with a reform of the appointments system, it argued, this would make the House representative of the country as a whole:

> The regions will all have a guaranteed place, while there will be a duty on the Appointments Commission to see that women and ethnic minorities and faith communities are also properly represented. And the hereditary element will finally be eliminated. (HM Government 2001: 35)

The proposal for reform of the House is thus to achieve a balance, having some members elected while preserving the attributes of the existing House. However, the most compelling argument is that embodied in the White Paper's conclusion. That is, that a balance of election and appointment is best suited to delivering a House that is representative. There are different meanings of representation (Pitkin 1967). Having elected members would mean that the House was representative in terms of being freely elected and acting on behalf of some individual or group (hence members 'representing' their constituencies). Appointing members would facilitate its being representative in terms of replicating the typical characteristics of a group or class (as in socio-economic background or ethnicity). Having a House that was representative solely in one sense could be at the expense of its being representative in another. Having a wholly elected membership could result in electors choosing members who, in terms of social and ethnic background, are atypical of the wider population.

By having a hybrid House, one cannot ensure that the House is wholly representative. Appointed members are, by definition, not freely elected and have no constituents to represent. Having members elected means that it is unlikely to be socially typical (unless one imposes quotas as to who can stand, thus restricting the choice of electors). However, one can seek to achieve at least some element of both, members of the public being able to elect some members to represent them and being able to see members appointed who may be drawn from the same or a similar background to their own. The government in its 2001 White Paper followed the Wakeham Commission in proposing that the Commission be required 'to ensure that the appointed members are broadly representative of British society' (HM Government 2001: 25). At least 30 per cent of the members should be women and 30 per cent men, with the Commission working towards gender balance over time. 'The Commission will also have regard to the importance of ensuring fair overall representation for both the nations and regions of the UK and from the ethnic minority communities' (HM Government 2001: 25).

The reform proposal can thus claim to be more comprehensive than the others in terms of embodying the different forms of representation. It also has a political benefit in that the appointed element can be employed to ensure not only that there is an independent element to the House, but also that no one party enjoys an overall majority. Having a minority of members elected militates against any one party gaining control of the House, thus protecting the effective fulfilment of the functions currently carried out by the House. There is general agreement among the parties – it is usually one of the prerequisites in considering the future of the House – that no one party should be in a position to control the House. By having a statutory Appointments Commission, operating independently and largely instead of prime ministerial patronage, it would be possible to ensure delivery of this goal.

Those favouring only partial election can find some support in the 2006 Populus poll cited in Chapter 3 which found that 75 per cent of respondents favoured a 'mainly' appointed House; the emphasis was on appointment, but the terminology did not exclude some elected members. In that poll, a reason for retaining mostly appointed members was embodied in the question. Polls tend to find that when people are offered options only as to the form that election should take, few support having only a few members elected. However, a House with equal numbers of elected and appointed members emerges in some polls with plurality support. Thus, for example, in the British Social Attitudes survey in 2007, 40 per cent of respondents supported 'appoint and elect equally', ahead of just under 28 per cent who favoured 'all or most elected'. Indeed, when we look at time series data (see Table 7.1) for the period from 2000 to 2010, the 'appoint and elected equally' option has been the most favoured for most of that period. Only in 2010 did the option of 'all or most elected' overtake it.

The reform approach thus constitutes an attempt to achieve some balance in terms of the different forms of representation, but a balance that can be characterised as cautious. It recognises the value of having some members of the second chamber elected, but is wary of jeopardising what it sees as the benefits deriving from the composition of the existing House. It achieved some prominence at the turn of the twenty-first century as a result of advocacy by the Wakeham Commission and broad acceptance of the Commission's recommendations by government. It has been somewhat overshadowed since by advocates of a largely or wholly elected chamber.

5

Replace

THE case for replacing the House of Lords with an elected chamber – or simply abolishing it (Chapter 6) – derives from seeing the House as illegitimate. As one Labour MP put it:

> any self-respecting democrat has to argue that its existence is an affront and that it cannot be allowed to continue. The idea that some citizens should be able to influence legislation by accident of birth or by occupation is unacceptable. It reinforces social class divisions ... It can thwart the intentions of a democratically elected government. (Garrett 1992: 171)

Critics of the House, as he noted, have veered between demanding its abolition and proposing a second chamber that is largely or wholly elected.

The argument that it should be elected, be it directly or indirectly (for example, with members drawn from other elected bodies, such as councils), has been made over a long period of time and by a range of individuals and bodies. The preamble to the Parliament Act 1911 declared, as we have noted (Chapter 3), that 'it is intended to substitute for the House of Lords as it presently exists a Second Chamber constituted on a popular instead of a hereditary basis', while noting that such substitution could not immediately be brought into operation.

For much of the century, proposals for replacing the existing membership of the House focused not so much on election by members of the public as on election by members of the House of Commons. In 1918 a report from an inter-party conference chaired by Lord Bryce, set up to consider the role and composition of the second chamber, recommended a House of 327 members, with 246 elected by MPs and the other 81 chosen by a joint committee of the two Houses. Various government committees, as well as the cabinet, considered the issue in the 1920s, but no agreement was reached on the proposal.

The idea of having members of the Lords elected by MPs was one that continued to be advanced well into the century. It was put forward by Harold Laski in 1947 in a foreword to a Fabian pamphlet, *Lords and Commons*, and endorsed in 1954 in another Fabian publication, *Reform of the Lords*, by Lord Chorley, Bernard Crick and Donald Chapman.

However, in the latter half of the century, calls for members of the second chamber to be elected by popular vote became more prominent. In 1977, Conservative politician Sir Ian Gilmour argued the case for a predominantly elected House (Gilmour 1977: 213–14). The following year, the Conservative Review Committee, chaired by former Prime Minister Lord Home, recommended a House of up to 402 members, with two-thirds elected (Conservative Review Committee 1978). A report the same year by the Constitutional Reform Committee of the Society of Conservative Lawyers was more radical, proposing a wholly elected House of 300 members, elected at staggered intervals (Society of Conservative Lawyers 1978). In 1981 Labour barrister (and later MP) Stuart Bell published a Fabian pamphlet arguing for an elected House of 328 members (Bell 1981). Conservative Action for Electoral Reform in 1983 also argued for a wholly elected House. Labour MP Graham Allen introduced a bill in 1989, 1990, and 1991 to provide for a directly elected House of 625 members, with one-third of the members elected every two years. Edward Heathcoat-Amory (1988) and William Wyndham (1998: 232), among other writers, also advocated a largely or wholly elected chamber. In 2002, a House of Commons Select Committee, the Public Administration Committee, entered the debate to advocate that 60 per cent of the members should be elected (Public Administration Committee 2002: 23).

Most of the proposals for a largely or wholly elected House came from individual politicians or from bodies set up by or allied to one of the political parties. Of the main political parties, only the Liberal Democrat Party (and previously the Liberal Party) had a policy favouring election of the second chamber. At its 1990 conference it advocated a 100-member Senate elected by the STV. However, advocacy of an elected House came to the fore in the twenty-first century, when all three principal parties embraced the principle of election.

Following the publication of the Labour government's White Paper in 2001 proposing that 20 per cent of members be elected, both the Conservative and Liberal Democrat parties published proposals in 2002 for a largely elected House. Both advocated a 300-member House, with 80 per cent of the members elected. As we have seen, following the votes of the House of Commons in 2007 that resulted in majorities for an 80 per cent and a 100 per cent elected House, the Labour leadership also swung behind supporting a largely elected chamber. Since 2007, all three main parties have thus favoured the 'replace' option.

We should also record that some politicians and commentators have proposed replacing the existing House not with a body of elected members, but with members selected at random or drawn from functional interests. Anthony Barnett and Peter Carty have advocated what they term the Athenian model, with members chosen by lot from the list of registered voters, but with regard being had to regional and gender balance (Barnett and Carty 2008). The method would thus be similar to selection for jury service, although in this case lasting longer – Barnett and Carty envisaged a maximum of four years' service.

Others have advocated a functional second chamber, that is, with members nominated by bodies such as trades unions, industry, and other sectional bodies. Winston Churchill came up with such a proposal in the 1930s (calling it an Economic Sub-Parliament), as did Labour MP John Mackintosh in the 1970s (Norton 1982: 29, 123–4). The case for such a chamber is that the representation of citizens by MPs in the House of Commons would be balanced by the representation of organised interests in the second chamber. This, it is argued, would enhance support for the political system through giving those interests a voice in the law-making process. Another proposal, advanced by Tony Benn (Anthony Wedgwood Benn as he was then known) in 1957, was for the Privy Council to replace the House of Lords as the second chamber (Benn 1957).

Our focus here, however, is primarily the case advanced for election. The objections levelled at selection by lot and at a functional chamber are the same as those levelled against the existing appointed chamber: that there is no direct accountability to electors.

There are two dimensions to the argument for replacing the House of Lords with an elected chamber. The first emphasises what is wrong with the current House and the other focuses on the merits of election. On the first, critics argue that the existing House is too large and has been prone to scandals (Gough 2009: 9). The House, as we have seen (Chapter 1), is second in size only to the Chinese National People's Congress. It has been subject to the several scandals in recent years. Some have encompassed the behaviour of peers, most notably 'cash for clauses', with some peers allegedly being willing to promote changes to legislation in return for payment, and others misusing the system of allowances. Two peers were imprisoned for claiming allowances to which they were not entitled. There was also a 'cash for peerages' scandal, an investigation in 2006–7 into claims that prime ministerial patronage had been employed in response to party donations.

These are problems with the existing House. By themselves, they are arguments for change, but not necessarily for election. The House has introduced rules designed to prevent a repetition of misbehaviour by members. However, the second dimension is the one stressed by advocates of replacement, namely that the House is not elected.

The House is seen as lacking the necessary legitimacy to fulfil its functions, not least to challenge effectively the government-dominated House of Commons. The members of the House are not accountable directly to electors and in most cases are in the House because of party patronage. The House is variously portrayed as the product of a bygone era, a charge levelled by Deputy Prime Minister Nick Clegg during discussions on reform in 2012. Media stories about the House are frequently accompanied by a picture of the State Opening of Parliament, showing peers in their ermine robes. Although this is the only time in the year that they wear the robes, it conveys a picture of a House steeped in tradition and detached from ordinary life.

Election is thus advocated on the grounds that it is the democratic option and would render members accountable to electors, either directly or indirectly, depending on the method of election employed. Accountability is at the heart of the argument. Supporters of election argue that those who are part of the law-making process should be accountable to the electorate for their decisions. Electing the members would generate public support and give members the confidence to challenge government. This, it is claimed, would not undermine the House of Commons but, rather, strengthen Parliament. The government would have to face two elected Houses, in one of which it might not have a majority. Most schemes for election of the second chamber are premised on a system that would likely deny any one party an overall majority.

Election would enhance the legitimacy of the second chamber, but would not necessarily render it equal with the House of Commons. Government would continue to be chosen through elections to the Commons. To ensure that an elected second chamber would not rival the legitimacy of the House of Commons, the Conservative Mackay Commission in 1999 recommended that one-third of members should be elected at each general election. This, it noted, would mean that only 30 per cent of the House 'would have a mandate as recent as that of the whole of the House of Commons' (Constitutional Commission on options for a new Second Chamber 1999: 35). Having six-member constituencies, it argued, would also mean that the link between members and constituents would be less specific than that between MP and constituents in the House of Commons.

A similar approach was adopted by the Labour government in 2008 in its White Paper, *An Elected Second Chamber: Further reform of the House of Lords*, designed to deliver on the previous year's vote in the Commons in favour of an elected second chamber. It too proposed staggered elections. 'Elections for the second chamber that were staggered over a number of electoral cycles could help ensure continued primacy of the House of Commons, as the latter would always have a more recent mandate than the second chamber taken as a whole' (HM Government 2008: 17). Like the Mackay Commission, it also recommended large constituencies.

In its White Paper the government also made the case for an appointed element, in order to 'preserve a significant independent element', echoing the recommendation of the Public Administration Committee (2002). It concluded:

> The presence of a significant minority of independent members would both distinguish the second chamber clearly from the House of Commons and complement the work of the Commons by providing non-partisan viewpoints in the legislative revision process. The size of any appointed element should be at the level of the 20% voted for by the House of Commons in March 2007. (HM Government 2008: 48)

The argument is that one would get the benefit of an independent element, but the very method of achieving it would mean that the second chamber could not match the House of Commons as a wholly elected chamber. It could not therefore make a claim to be co-equal. At the same time, having appointed members comprise only a minority of the second chamber would mean that they were not seen as a threat to the enhanced legitimacy of the newly invigorated chamber. They could be outvoted by the elected members and, as tends to be the case with independent members, might not be as assiduous in voting as party members are. Their voices could inform debate, but their votes would be unlikely to determine the outcomes.

A largely elected House would thus, it is argued, not challenge the primacy of the Commons, but would be more confident in calling government to account. It could both counter a government-dominated House of Commons as well as alleviate some of the burdens on MPs. According to two leading Conservatives, Kenneth Clarke and Sir George Young (now Lord Young of Cookham):

> the dominance of the majority party of the day, coupled with other demands on MPs' time from constituency casework, put some limits on the Commons' ability to perform a scrutinising and revising role. It is this role that a second chamber, differently constituted from the Commons, should discharge. Even though the current House of Lords is increasingly effective, we believe that only a democratic mandate can entrench the position of a second chamber. (Gough 2009: 8)

Some supporters of election take a more purist view in that they advocate a wholly elected House. The argument here is that this would ensure the legitimacy of the whole House, not just a majority who are elected, and would embolden the House in fulfilling the functions ascribed to it. Elections, it is argued, may and do produce members who are well versed in various fields – the Commons may at times be just as well informed as the Lords on some issues (see Bochel and Defty 2010: 66–84). Electoral systems can be devised to facilitate the return of independent members or, at least, members who are chosen on their own merits and because of their independent stance within parties. (This is one of the arguments advanced for the STV system.) The House could be more confident in challenging the executive and inviting the Commons to think again. The Commons would remain the dominant chamber, given that government would be chosen through it, and members of the second chamber would seek election knowing that their role, if elected, was different.

Advocates of replacement thus focus on input legitimacy. They believe that the functions of the House of Lords are appropriate, and have no wish to change them. Rather, they see an elected chamber as a body that would not so much challenge these functions as enable them to be fulfilled more effectively.

However, it is possible to advocate an elected House on the grounds that election would, and *should*, affect the functions and powers of the House. The debate on the future of the Lords is premised largely on the desirability of maintaining a system of asymmetrical bicameralism, ensuring an effective system of government. The government with an overall majority of seats in the Commons can ultimately get its programme of public policy enacted. There is thus what Lord Hailsham once charac- terised as an elective dictatorship (Hailsham 1976). Why should there not be a second chamber able to withstand, and not simply to challenge (as most advocates of the replace option prefer), the will of a government-dominated House of Commons?

One can make a case for dispersing power through greater symmetry in the nation's cameral arrangements, generating a House that is more akin to a co-equal chamber and able to challenge the government-dominated House of Commons. Why should not an elected chamber be able to say 'no' to the other elected chamber and make it stick? This would be a means of limiting government. If the members were to be elected from the different parts of the United Kingdom, one could have what would amount to the equivalent of second chambers in federal nations, speaking for the different components that make up the nation.

This more radical view can be seen as deriving from a liberal view of the constitution (Norton 1982: 275–9), favouring the protection of individual liberty through a dispersal of power. The more dominant view, based on retaining a system of asym- metrical bicameralism, derives from a more traditional model, the Westminster model of government (Norton 1982: 279–87), wishing to retain accountability through election to the House of Commons.

This radical view thus provides a different case for election than that advanced by parties and government. However, it has not figured prominently in debate. As we have seen, the proposals brought forward by successive governments are based on the second chamber's remaining one that fulfils tasks complementary to those of the House of Commons. That has underpinned parliamentary debate, and it informed the draft House of Lords Reform Bill introduced by the coalition government in 2012.

In arguing their case, supporters of election are able to call on the aid of public opinion. When offered a choice between an appointed and an elected House, respondents opt for the latter. In 2012, when asked how they would vote in a referendum if the choice were between electing at least 80 per cent of the members or continuing with the present arrangements, 69 per cent supported election, against 23 per cent favouring the existing system of appointment.

When the options include abolition and equal numbers of appointed and elected peers, the all or mostly elected option generally gains plurality support. In some polls, there is a clear majority if the all-elected and mostly elected options are combined. An ICM poll in 2001, for example, found that 27 per cent of respondents supported a wholly elected House and 27 per cent supported a mostly elected House, hence a majority – 54 per cent – favouring a mostly or wholly elected House. A YouGov poll in 2003 found a similar majority of 55 per cent, with 33 per cent expressing support for a wholly elected House and 22 per cent for a mostly elected House. The percentage was down to 49 per cent in a 2012 YouGov poll, but it still represented the plurality view, the percentage of 'Don't knows' having increased to 22 per cent and constituting the second-largest response, ahead of 20 per cent who favoured equal numbers of appointed and elected members.

Proponents of a largely or wholly elected chamber have tended to make the running in debate in recent years, with their views being embraced in the twenty-first century by the leaders of the main political parties and by successive governments. They can point to public support at least for the principle of election and have seen a government bill introduced in 2012 to provide for a largely elected House. What they have not yet managed to do is mobilise sufficient political support to get such a measure onto the statute book. As we shall see, they encounter two problems. Support for an elected House may be broad, but it is not deep, and moving from principle to agreed detail is, if not an insuperable hurdle, at least one that has not yet been overcome.

6

Remove altogether

THE UK is distinctive, although not unique, in having a second chamber. As we have noted (Chapter 1), most nations have unicameral legislatures. Indeed, this is also now a feature of legislatures within the United Kingdom: the Scottish Parliament, the National Assembly for Wales, and the Northern Ireland Assembly are single-chamber legislatures. (The Northern Ireland Parliament that existed from 1922 to 1972 was bicameral.) Although some parliaments are created as unicameral when a nation is first formed, some established nations, such as New Zealand, have made the shift from a bicameral to a unicameral legislature. Some politicians argue that the UK should follow the example of New Zealand.

Some favour abolition on principle – they see no grounds for a second chamber – and others favour abolition in preference to an elected chamber. The latter focus on maintaining the primacy of the House of Commons and believe that the election of a second chamber would challenge that primacy in a way that an appointed chamber cannot. For them, their first preference is an appointed House. Abolition is the default if the government seeks to achieve an elected chamber.

Our primary focus is those who believe in abolition on principle. Various politicians on the Left have made the case for unicameralism. Michael Foot led opposition to the Parliament (No. 2) Bill in 1969 on the grounds that he was, as he put it, 'a fervent abolitionist' (*House of Commons Debates*, 3 February 1969, col. 90).

In 1976, Labour backbencher Dennis Skinner sought leave to introduce a bill to abolish the House of Lords. The motion was defeated by 15 votes. The following year, the Labour Party conference supported abolition. The party's National Executive Committee (NEC) declared that the House of Lords 'was an outmoded institution, completely inappropriate to a modern democratic system of government'.

The policy of abolition was confirmed by the Party's 1980 conference. At that conference, Tony Benn said that within three months of a Labour government being elected it should introduce three major pieces of legislation. These were an Industry bill (extending public ownership), a bill to transfer all powers back from the Common Market to the House of Commons, and immediate abolition of the House of Lords (Cocks 1989: 74–5). The same year saw another attempt, this time by Labour MP Jeff Rooker, to introduce a bill to abolish the House. (This time the motion was defeated by 98 votes.) In 1984, Tony Benn introduced a Reform Bill to provide that the House of Lords would cease to exist on the day the Act came into force. The functions of the House would transfer to the House of Commons, except for the judicial function, which would transfer to the Privy Council.

The case for abolition has continued to be pressed by a number of MPs, especially although not exclusively Labour MPs. In the votes in the House of Commons in 2003, 172 MPs – more than one-quarter of all MPs – voted for an amendment opposing the appointed option on the grounds that it did not provide for a unicameral legislature. In 2007, 163 MPs voted against retaining a bicameral legislature.

The case for abolition derives from one of two perspectives: that the House, as a second chamber, is pointless or is objection-able. These two perspectives address a conundrum at the heart of bicameralism in the UK, which was encapsulated in the pithy observation of the Abbé Sieyès: 'If a Second Chamber dissents from the First, it is mischievous; if it agrees, it is superfluous' (McKechnie 1909: 96). Lord Wedderburn put it slightly differently, getting to the heart of the second perspective when he declared:

'Either the second chamber is less democratic than the Commons in which case it should not be able to delay legislation, or it is just as democratic, when there is no point in having two chambers' (quoted in Herbert 1979).

The first objection, then, is essentially a practical one. If the second chamber duplicates the first or simply endorses what it says, there is little point in its existence. Its justification rests on the fact that it fulfils functions that are distinctive and add value to the political process. It seeks to fulfil its tasks without challenging the primacy of the first chamber. In so far as it is in a position to challenge the Commons, and especially if it does challenge what MPs have done, then it becomes objectionable on democratic grounds.

Labour politicians have tended to be to the fore in objecting to the existence of the House of Lords, given that until 1999 it had a Conservative bias and was therefore more likely to create problems for a Labour government than for a Conservative one. Although the House occasionally defeated a Conservative government over amendments to bills, the number of defeats was well below that suffered by Labour administrations. In the 1974–79 Parliament, the Labour government suffered 347 defeats at the hands of their Lordships, compared with 45 defeats in the 1979–83 Parliament under a Conservative government (Norton 1985: 14). It is perhaps not surprising, therefore, that during the period of Labour government in the 1970s, the Labour Party embraced the policy of abolishing the second chamber.

Although the Conservative bias was removed as a consequence of the House of Lords Act 1999, the House remains able to challenge the elected House. Some Labour politicians remain wary, given that second chambers have a reputation for being conservative bodies. The Conservative government returned in 2015 also found itself encountering problems in the House, not least over secondary legislation on tax credits.

The objection to the House's seeking to frustrate the will of the elected House is that it is an appointed House. If it were partly elected (that is, the reform rather than the replace option), a similar objection would apply, given that it could not claim the same legitimacy as the wholly elected first chamber. If it were a wholly elected House, then it could claim to be as legitimate as the first chamber and, indeed, depending on the electoral system by which members were chosen, might try to sustain a claim to be more legitimate. On the face of it, having two elected chambers would seem to be democratic, if democracy is equated solely with election, but not democratic if one takes democracy to be how people choose to govern themselves.

As we have seen (Chapter 3), accountability may be deemed to be core to a system of representative democracy. Having two elected chambers clashing with one another, producing no outcome or outcomes that are compromises at variance with the preferences of the people, undermines accountability. There is no body to be held to account for what has happened. In this respect, those who favour retaining an appointed House and supporters of abolition are united in finding such a situation objectionable. Abolitionists, though, have a claim that having a unicameral legislature is, in democratic terms, the pristine option. Having one chamber alone would ensure that there was core accountability. As Colin Tyler has written, although not advocating abolition: 'Of course, another option would be to abolish the Lords completely. The resulting unicameral system *would* be more democratic than the present system' (Tyler 2012: 200). There would be nothing to challenge the people's representatives assembled in the one chamber.

There is a practical objection in that it would be difficult for the House of Commons to cope with the consequences, either shouldering an additional burden or losing the benefits accruing from the work of the Lords. According to William Wyndham, 'Abolition of the Lords would at least ensure reform of the Commons. Only a little less certainly it would result also in the formation of a Second Chamber soon afterwards' (Wyndham 1998: 135). Supporters of bicameralism point out that it tends to be small nations that have unicameral legislatures. Larger democracies, it is argued, would have difficulty coping with only one chamber, given usually the volume of legislation. Removing one chamber would also remove an important body for scrutinising and constraining the executive, dominant as it usually is in the House of Commons.

Abolitionists have responded to this argument by claiming that it does not create an insuperable hurdle. In 1978 the Labour Party NEC said that the problem could be met by reforming the House of Commons and by the development of other means of scrutinising bills, such as the establishment of a special select committee to consider bills after they had received a third reading. The abolitionists' argument is that experts should be on tap and not on top and be available to appear before or advise committees in the legislature. 'The notion that we cannot do away with the House of Lords because of the revising requirements', declared Michael Foot during debate on the Parliament (No. 2) Bill, 'is quite wrong. We could remodel the life of Parliament itself so as to deal with these problems. It might take a little time to do that, but it could be done' (*House of Commons Debates*, 3 February 1969, col. 90). In 2012 Tony Benn argued the case for a national advisory committee – comprising 'a representative gathering of people from different parts of our society' – to look at legislation and make recommendations to the Commons. 'To do this would be to abolish the House of Lords altogether and start afresh in a way that was useful and constructive' (Benn 2012).

There is also a legal problem in that Parliament constitutes for law-making purposes the Queen-in-Parliament, and Parliament comprises the House of Commons and the House of Lords. Abolishing the House of Lords could mean that the courts no longer recognised the doctrine of parliamentary sovereignty if what constituted Parliament for the purposes of the doctrine no longer existed. If an Act to abolish the House was passed under the provisions of the Parliament Acts, the Commons would be using the procedures of the Acts to destroy the very procedure that was established by the Acts. It is possible that the courts would refuse to recognise such an Act and subsequent Acts passed without reference to the House of Lords (Mirfield 1979: 36–58).

This interpretation, however, has been disputed. George Winterton has argued that there is nothing to prevent the

Commons using the Parliament Acts to remove the Lords from the provisions of those Acts. Moreover, he argued, the Lords could be abolished *de facto* by abolishing the peerage system so as to leave the House without members, or by amending the Parliament Acts to provide that bills receive Royal Assent immediately after they have been passed by the House of Commons (Winterton 1979: 386–92).

Advocates of abolition cannot claim that their stance enjoys majority support among the public. Nonetheless, in polls on the future of the second chamber, the proportion of respondents who favour abolition is not insignificant. On occasion, in the British Social Attitudes Survey, the percentage has exceeded 20 per cent. (As we shall see in Table 7.1, it reached 22 per cent in 2010.) An Angus Reid poll in 2010 (Table 6.1) found 30 per cent of respondents favouring a unicameral legislature. Another poll by Angus Reid the following year put the figure at 28 per cent, slightly below the figure of 2010 but nonetheless showing that

Table 6.1   House of Lords Reform

Now we'd like to ask you some questions about the House of Lords. Which of these statements comes closest to your own point of view?

The UK does not need a House of Lords, all legislation should be reviewed and authorised by the House of Commons.	30%
The UK needs a House of Lords, but the people should be allowed to take part in the process to choose Lords.	40%
The UK needs a House of Lords, and the current guidelines that call for appointed Lords should not be modified.	9%
Not sure.	21%

Source: Angus Reid, October 2010

more than a quarter of those questioned saw no need for a second chamber.

Abolition of the second chamber is the most radical of the four approaches. Some politicians see a case for a second chamber, but – as we have mentioned – would support abolition in preference to an elected House that was in a position to challenge the primacy of the House of Commons. Others have a principled objection to the second chamber and their stance is not contingent on changes to the House of Lords. For them, a unicameral legislature is a desirable goal.

7

The future of the second chamber

THE House of Lords has been much discussed, but the debate
has been characterised by heat rather than light. There have been
two notable deficiencies in the debate. The first is that in terms
of popular debate it is rarely derived from first principles.

It is not unusual to find people offering their schemes of
reform detached from any prior discussion of the principles
underpinning those schemes. As Janet Morgan once observed:

> On summer evenings and winter afternoons, when they
> have nothing else to do, people discuss how to reform the
> House of Lords. Schemes are taken out of cupboards and
> drawers and dusted off; speeches are composed, pamphlets
> written, letters sent to the newspapers. From time to time,
> the whole country becomes excited. (Morgan 1981: 18)

However, the letters written to newspapers, or sent to parliamentar-
ians, tend to detail schemes of composition – 30 per cent of the
membership should be selected by learned societies, 20 per cent
nominated by charities, and the like. In short, in Morgan's words,
the focus has been on 'how to reform' rather than 'why reform?'
The schemes are not so much the end point, deriving from clearly
stated principles but, rather, the starting point of the contributions.
Some make no mention of principles and take them as given.
Electing the second chamber is frequently taken as self-evidently
the democratic option. It is not unusual to see reference to 'a
democratically elected' second chamber, although no one appears
to be advancing a case for an undemocratically elected chamber.

Electing the second chamber, as we have seen (Chapter 3), does not necessarily translate into a democratic system of government but, rather, can be taken to challenge it.

This problem is marked in popular debate, and less so in government contributions to the debate on the future of the second chamber. Government proposals, embodied in white papers, typically state the principles that underpin the proposals. However, on occasion the principles enunciated are not always obviously compatible, not least in seeking to retain the existing experience and expertise of the House while also injecting electoral legitimacy. However, the challenge for governments is arguably even greater in respect of the second problem, namely that the House of Lords is discussed in isolation from the rest of the political system.

We have quoted Colin Tyler making the point that 'ultimately it is the democratic character of Parliament that matters, not the democratic character of its constituent parts considered in isolation from each other' (Tyler 2012: 200). The key point here is that it is rare to consider Parliament as Parliament. Each House is considered in isolation. The term 'parliamentary reform' tends to refer to the House of Commons and encompass structural and procedural change. 'Lords reform' is distinct and deals, as we have seen, with the composition of the House. There is no thinking about Parliament as Parliament and no thinking about the role of Parliament within the constitution of the United Kingdom. As academic and politician David Howarth put it:

> We have no structural thinking going on about the interaction between the composition of the Houses [of Parliament], the electoral systems, the courts and so on. We have no thinking about how all this fits together into a system of government. (Constitution Committee 2011: 13)

Constitutional reform in the UK has taken place in recent decades, especially in the years since 1997, on a substantial scale, but the changes derive from no intellectually coherent approach to constitutional change. There are different approaches (Norton 1982: 261–94), but reforms that have been implemented by successive governments derive from none of them. They have been implemented as disparate and discrete measures, justified on their individual merits, rather than deriving from a clear articulation of a particular type of constitution deemed most suitable for the United Kingdom (Norton 2007b: 119–20). The Labour government of Tony Blair implemented a raft of major constitutional changes, but the Prime Minister had little interest in them and the Lord Chancellor, Lord Irvine of Lairg, admitted that the government proceeded not only on the basis of no 'all-embracing theory', but also without an all-embracing definition of a constitution (*House of Lords Debates*, 18 December 2002, col. 642). The coalition government formed in 2010 was composed of two parties that, on constitutional issues, adopted approaches to constitutional change that were at different ends of the spectrum (Norton 2015: 472).

The absence of any intellectually coherent approach to constitutional change is apparent in respect of attempts to change the House of Lords. The House of Lords Bill was introduced in 1999 essentially as a free-standing measure to remove hereditary peers from the House. It was not related to other measures of constitutional reform or set within a clear view of constitutional change. The government set up the Wakeham Commission to advise it as to what to do next. After failing to get much support for its proposals for a House with 20 per cent of members elected, it effectively hived the issue off to a joint committee of the two Houses. (After the inconclusive votes in the Commons on the different options in 2003, the joint committee basically put the issue back to government.) After the votes in the Commons in 2007, the government decided to give effect to the vote for a largely elected House.

The debate is thus characterised by a lack of integrated thinking within government about the nation's constitutional arrangements. The future of the House of Lords is not set within a clear view of the type of constitution deemed most appropriate for the United Kingdom.

The debate is characterised also by another, rather prominent and practical problem: the lack of consensus. As one senior peer,

Lord Denham, once observed, if you put four people in a room to discuss the future of the House of Lords, you get five different answers (Norton 1982: 130). The absence of any clear majority view is borne out by survey data. Time series data from the British Social Attitudes Survey shows the different views (Table 7.1). Support has mobilised behind no single approach. Each enjoys minority support.

Indeed, attitudes towards the future of the House are characterised not only by diversity but also by confusion. Members of the public hold views that are incompatible. We have drawn

Table 7.1   What should happen to the House of Lords?

About the House of Lords. Which of these statements come closest to your view about what should happen to the House of Lords?	2000	2002	2005	2007	2010
All or most of its members should be appointed	5.4%	4.8%	7.0%	7.2%	5.9%
All or most elected	28.9%	30.9%	26.2%	27.8%	31.2%
Appoint and elect equally	32.5%	35.0%	35.3%	40.1%	28.1%
It should be abolished	20.9%	18.3%	17.9%	13.2%	22.1%
Don't know	12.0%	10.8%	13.5%	11.6%	11.8%
Not answered	0.3%	0.2%	0.1%	0.1%	0.8%

Source: British Social Attitude Survey Database; 28th British Social Attitudes Report.

attention (Chapter 3) to the Populus poll in 2006 that found that a majority of respondents wanted *both* 'a mainly appointed house' and one in which 'at least half of the members ... should be elected'. The responses are shown in full in Table 7.2, which highlights even more the internally conflicting views that are held. A majority of those questioned favour most members being elected, but accept that if both Houses were elected it would be difficult to get things done and would bring the prospect of frequent stalemate.

The responses are revealing in that they draw out the desire to retain the existing strengths of the House derived from appointment, while wishing to accord electoral legitimacy to the House. The Populus survey provides some succour for the retain, reform, and replace options, while at the same time challenging each. Supporters of retaining an appointed chamber can point to the largest majority being in favour of retaining a largely appointed House. Supporters of the replace option can call in aid the fact that almost three-quarters of respondents recognise the case for most members being elected. Proponents of the reform option could argue that they, in effect, seek to meet the desire to retain experience and expertise, while also injecting some electoral legitimacy, although clearly falling short in terms of the proportion to be elected.

Furthermore, that lack of consensus is to be found within particular approaches. Among those favouring an elected House, there is disagreement as to the form of election. The problem was neatly encapsulated in the government's 2008 White Paper, *An Elected Second Chamber: Further reform of the House of Lords*:

> The Government proposes that members of the second chamber should be elected directly. There was not consensus about the system that should be used for such elections. The Conservative Party favours a First Past The Post system. The Liberal Democrats favour the use of an open list or Single Transferable Vote system. The Government believes that further consideration should be given to the options of using either First Past The Post, Alternative Vote, Single Transferable Vote (STV), open or semi-open list system. (HM Government 2008: 15)

Table 7.2 Options for the future of the House of Lords

The main political parties are currently debating further reform of the House of Lords. Please say whether you agree or disagree with	Agree	Disagree	Refused	Don't know
It is important to have a strong House of Lords to serve as a check on the House of Commons and the Government.	78%	17%	3%	5%
It is right that the House of Commons can ultimately overrule the House of Lords because the Commons is elected and the Lords is not.	62%	28%	3%	9%
The House of Lords should remain a mainly appointed house because this gives it a degree of independence from electoral politics and allows people with a broad range of experience and expertise to be involved in the law-making process.	75%	19%	1%	6%
At least half the members of the House of Lords should be elected so that the upper chamber of Parliament has democratic legitimacy.	72%	21%	1%	7%
If both Houses of Parliament were elected it would become much harder for governments to get things done since both Houses could claim democratic legitimacy and neither would be willing to back down, bringing the risk of frequent stalemate.	56%	33%	<1%	10%

Source: Populus, April 2006.

Reaching agreement on the first statement, that there should be a second chamber elected by direct election, is, as we have seen, difficult, but the point here is that it constitutes the start and not the end of a process. The choice of electoral system is far from agreed, even within government. As we have seen, the coalition government in 2012 switched from STV in its draft bill to a regional list in the bill that it introduced. Nor is it a matter of incidental detail. Institutions and processes are not neutral in their effect. Selecting one electoral system over another can have profound implications for the outcome, and hence the very nature of the body being elected.

It is possible also to distinguish between an inchoate debate as to what *should* happen to the House of Lords and the circumstances of political life that may determine what *will* happen to it. We can distinguish within the latter between being in Opposition and being in government.

Opposition leaders in recent years have variously advocated an elected second chamber as a way of brandishing their democratic credentials. Critics have suggested that the motivation may instead be because it is largely a cost-free policy in economic terms. In terms of coming up with policy proposals, it constitutes what may be called 'low hanging fruit'. It was a policy adopted by successive Conservative leaders in Opposition, starting with William Hague. Labour under Ed Miliband also supported an elected House and voted for the second reading of the House of Lords Reform Bill in 2012 (although not the motion to programme it). Labour leader Jeremy Corbyn, under challenge for the Labour leadership in 2016, argued the case for a wholly elected second chamber as part of a package of democratic renewal.

The situation is less clear cut in government. If we look at the period since the start of the twentieth century, it is notable that none of the changes brought about by legislation since 1911 has been the product of a clearly articulated view of constitutional change. Governments have variously approached the issue in a response mode, as in 1911, 1949, 1963, and in 2000 following enactment of the House of Lords Act 1999. Even in the debate leading to the 1911 Parliament Act, there was little debate about the role of the second chamber as such in the political process (Norton 2013: 168). The major reform proposal of the twenty-first century, the House of Lords Reform Bill, was the result of compromise. Although both the Conservative and Liberal Democrats favoured an elected second chamber, they disagreed as to the political saliency of the issue and the means to achieve it. For the Liberal Democrats, it was one of their treasured goals. For the Conservatives, the party leader, David Cameron, had made clear in the previous Parliament that he regarded it as a 'third term issue'; in other words, although formally committed to an elected House, he would not be taking any action to achieve it in the foreseeable future. The parties differed on the form of electoral system to be used. The bill was introduced in 2012 with little enthusiasm on the part of many Conservatives. As we have seen (Chapter 2), it was opposed by a substantial body of Conservative MPs and effectively derailed by the Labour Opposition's failing to support a timetable for its passage.

The future of the House of Lords is thus difficult to discern with any certainty. All three main political parties acquired leaders in the twenty-first century committed to an elected second chamber, but that does not presage action on the issue. The commitment of the Prime Minister to change may be necessary, but it is not sufficient. A commitment in principle is not the same as a commitment to action. Reform may be supported, but not accorded priority. When in July 2016 an e-petition to Parliament calling for removal of Church of England bishops from the House of Lords closed with 15,793 signatures (sufficient to elicit a government response), the government replied: 'Changes to the composition of the House of Lords, including Church of England Bishops, are important but, given the very full programme of other constitutional changes, are not a priority at present.'

The new Conservative Prime Minister in 2016, Theresa May, had previously voted for an elected House. She was on the ministerial committee in coalition responsible for the draft House of Lords Reform Bill. However, the reason for her becoming Prime Minister, namely David Cameron's resignation following the result of the June 2016 referendum on the UK's membership of the European Union, provided her with other priorities.

Conclusion

This narrative has drawn out the problems inherent in trying to discern the future of the House of Lords. What we can say, based on the foregoing, is:

1   There is general, though not universal, acceptance of the proposition that the second chamber should fulfil functions that complement the first chamber (which should remain the principal House) and that these are functions fulfilled by the House of Lords.

2   There is support, usually plurality support, for some members of the second chamber to be elected; few polls, when presented solely with options, show support for retaining a wholly appointed chamber.

3   In the event of a choice between fulfilling effectively the existing functions of the House of Lords and having elected members, people tend to prefer the former to the latter. Supporters of an appointed chamber contend that this is a real choice – it is an either/or option – whereas supporters of a largely or wholly elected House believe that they are not mutually exclusive.

4   Change to the second chamber will generally elicit popular support when prompted, but rarely generates unsolicited activity and enthusiasm. Although in surveys 20 to 30 per cent of respondents support abolition of the House of Lords, in 2015 a parliamentary e-petition calling for abolition closed after the stipulated period of six months having gathered only 2,976 signatures. It is not unusual for MPs to point out that no one has mentioned the issue of Lords' reform on the doorstep when they have been canvassing.

5   Changes to the House of Lords are more likely to be incremental, affecting the procedures, powers, and membership within an appointed House (as was the case with the private

members' bills in the 2010–15 Parliament), rather than radical. Any legislation to introduce an element of election is more likely to fall foul of a lack of consensus and be squeezed out by other government priorities.

The priorities are reflected in petitions submitted to Parliament. Whereas a petition to abolish the House of Lords attracted fewer than 3,000 signatures, one calling for a threshold to be applied (in effect retrospectively) to the referendum on EU membership attracted more than 4.4 million signatures. The petitions reflect also the relative attention to the Houses afforded by the public. Of more than 21,000 petitions submitted online to Parliament by the summer of 2016, few covered Parliament itself, and of those that did the one attracting most support (in excess of 100,000 signatures) was one calling for MPs to sit on Saturdays.

This is not to argue that a measure to introduce a largely or wholly elected second chamber will not be introduced or make it to the statute book. As we have seen, a measure to create a largely elected House was introduced by government in 2012: the likelihood of that happening was not envisaged even two years before. What that experience showed was that the bill was the product of political forces at work, rather than a measure emanating from a clear, intellectually coherent view of constitutional change. In that, there was nothing new – major constitutional change in the UK is rarely the product of prior reflection and cross-party consensus (Norton 2011b: 15–16). Given the inchoate nature of debate on the UK constitution in the twenty-first century, that is likely to remain the case.

The history of the House of Lords is one of institutional continuity and occasional seminal and more frequent incremental change, with none of the changes resulting from a clear, considered view of the role of the House of Lords, let alone the role of Parliament, in the constitution of the United Kingdom. That appears unlikely to change.

Further reading

THE principal works on the House of Lords are Emma Crewe, *Lords of Parliament* (Manchester: Manchester University Press, 2005), Donald Shell, *The House of Lords*, 2nd edn (Manchester: Manchester University Press, 2007) and Meg Russell, *The Contemporary House of Lords* (Oxford: Oxford University Press, 2013). On the work of the House, prior to the reforms of 1999, see Donald Shell and David Beamish (eds), *The House of Lords at Work* (Oxford: Clarendon Press, 1993) and Paul Carmichael and Bryce Dickson (eds), *The House of Lords: Its Parliamentary and Judicial Roles* (Oxford: Hart Publishing, 1999). The classic study of the House prior to the introduction of life peers is Peter A. Bromhead, *The House of Lords and Contemporary Politics* (London: Routledge and Kegan Paul, 1958).

On reform of the House, the main works are Meg Russell, *Reforming the House of Lords: Lessons from Overseas* (Oxford: Oxford University Press, 2000), Chris Ballinger, *The House of Lords 1911–2011* (Oxford: Hart Publishing, 2011) and Peter Dorey and Alex Kelso, *House of Lords Reform since 1911* (Basingstoke: Palgrave Macmillan, 2011). A useful short history is Lord Longford, *A History of the House of Lords* (London: Collins, 1988).

The principal documents on reform are drawn together in four volumes, Peter Raina (ed.), *House of Lords Reform: A History* (Oxford: Peter Lang), Vol. I: The Origins to 1937 (2011), Vol. 2: 1943–1958: Hopes Rekindled (2013), Vol. 3: 1960–1969: Reforms Attempted (2014), Vol. 4, 1971–2014: The Exclusion of the Hereditary Peers (2015).

References

Baldwin, Nicholas D. J. (1985), 'The House of Lords: Behavioural Changes', in Philip Norton (ed.), *Parliament in the 1980s*, Oxford: Basil Blackwell.

Baldwin, Nicholas D. J. (1993), 'The Membership of the House', in Donald Shell and David Beamish (eds), *The House of Lords at Work*, Oxford: Clarendon Press, 1993.

Barnett, Anthony and Carty, Peter (2008), *The Athenian Option*, London: Imprint Academic.

Bell, Stuart (1981), *How to Abolish the Lords*, London: The Fabian Society.

Benn, Anthony Wedgwood (1957), *The Privy Council as a Second Chamber*, London: The Fabian Society.

Benn, Tony (2012), 'We should abolish the Lords, not reform it', *New Statesman*, 12 July.

Bochel, Hugh and Defty, Andrew (2010), 'A Question of Expertise: the House of Lords and Welfare Policy', *Parliamentary Affairs*, Vol. 27(1): 66–84.

Bromhead, Peter A. (1958), *The House of Lords and Contemporary Politics*, London: Routledge and Kegan Paul.

Chorley, Lord, Crick, Bernard and Chapman, Donald (1954), *Reform of the Lords*, London: Fabian Publications.

Cocks, Michael (1989), *Labour and the Benn Factor*, London: Macdonald.

Conservative Review Committee (1978), *The House of Lords*, London: Conservative Central Office.

Constitution Committee, House of Lords (2011), *The Process of Constitutional Change*, 15th Report, Session 2010–12, HL Paper 177.

Constitutional Commission on options for a new Second Chamber (1999), *The Report of the Constitutional Commission on options for a new Second Chamber*, London: The Constitutional Commission.

Crewe, Emma (2005), *Lords of Parliament*, Manchester: Manchester University Press.

Dicey, A. V. (1885), *Introduction to the Study of the Law of the Constitution*, London: Macmillan.

European Union Committee, House of Lords (2016a), *The process of withdrawing from the European Union*, 11th Report, Session 2015–16, HL Paper 138.

European Union Committee, House of Lords (2016b), *Scrutinising Brexit: the role of Parliament*, 1st Report, Session 2016–17, HL Paper 33.

Forsyth, Michael (2012), 'Constitutional Reform', in Lord Howard of Rising (ed.), *Enoch at 100*, London: Biteback Publishing.

Fox, Ruth and Blackwell, Joel (2014), *The Devil Is in the Detail: Parliament and Delegated Legislation*, London: The Hansard Society.

Garrett, John (1992), *Westminster: Does Parliament Work?* London: Victor Gollancz.

Gilmour, Ian (1977), *Inside Right: A Study of Conservatism*, London: Hutchinson.

Gough, Roger (2009) (ed.) *An Elected Second Chamber: A Conservative View*, London: The Constitution Unit.

Grantham, Cliff and Moore Hodgson, Caroline (1985), 'The House of Lords: Structural Changes', in Philip Norton (ed.), *Parliament in the 1980s*, Oxford: Basil Blackwell.

Hailsham, Lord (1976), *Elective Dictatorship*, London: BBC.

Heathcoat-Amory, Edward (1988), *Lords A' Leaping*, London: Centre for Policy Studies.

Herbert, Hugh (1979), 'The Lords under the Microscope', *Guardian*, 1 March.

Hibbing, John R. and Theiss-Morse, Elizabeth (1995), *Congress as Public Enemy*, Cambridge: Cambridge University Press.

HM Government (2001), *The House of Lords: Completing the Reform*, Cm 5291, London: The Stationery Office.

HM Government (2007), *The Governance of Britain*, Cm. 7170, London: The Stationery Office.

HM Government (2008), *An Elected Second Chamber: Further reform of the House of Lords*, Cm. 7438, London: The Stationery Office.

HM Government (2011), *House of Lords Reform Draft Bill*, Cm 8077, London: The Stationery Office.

Hunt, Murray, Hooper, Hayley and Yowell, Paul (2012), *Parliament and Human Rights: Redressing the Democratic Deficit*, Swindon: Arts and Humanities Research Council.

Jenkins, Roy (1954), *Mr Balfour's Poodle*, London: Heinemann.

Kelso, Alexandra (2006), 'Reforming the House of Lords: Navigating Representation, Democracy and Legitimacy at Westminster', *Parliamentary Affairs*, Vol. 59: 563–81.

King, Anthony (1981), 'The Rise of the Career Politician in Britain – and Its Consequences', *British Journal of Political Science*, Vol. 11: 249–85.

Laski, Harold (1947), 'Foreword', in Frank Hardie and Robert S. W. Pollard, *Lords and Commons*, London: Fabian Publications.

Le Seuer, Andrew and Simpson Caird, Jack (2013), 'The House of Lords Select Committee on the Constitution', in Alexander Horne, Gavin Drewry and Dawn Oliver (eds), *Parliament and the Law*, Oxford: Hart Publishing.

Longford, Lord (1988), *A History of the House of Lords*, London: Collins.

McKechnie, William Sharp (1909), *The Reform of the House of Lords*, Glasgow: James MacLehose & Sons.

McKenzie, Kenneth (1968), *The English Parliament*, London: Penguin.

MacLean, Stephen (2011), 'Public Choice Theory and House of Lords Reform', *Economic Affairs*, Vol. 31 (3): 46–8.

Massicotte, Louis (2001), 'Legislative Unicameralism: A Global Survey and a Few Case Studies', *The Journal of Legislative Studies*, Vol. 7(1): 151–70.

Mirfield, Peter (1979), 'Can the House of Lords Lawfully be Abolished?' *Law Quarterly Review*, Vol. 95: 36–58.

Morgan, Janet (1975), *The House of Lords and the Labour Government 1964–1970*, Oxford: Clarendon Press.

Morgan, Janet (1981), 'The House of Lords in the 1980s', *The Parliamentarian*, Vol. 62(1): 18–26.

Natzler, David and Millar, Douglas (1993), 'Private Members' Bills', in Donald Shell and David Beamish (eds), *The House of Lords at Work*, Oxford: Clarendon Press, 1993.

Norton, Philip (1981), *The Commons in Perspective*, Oxford: Martin Robertson.

Norton, Philip (1982), *The Constitution in Flux*, Oxford: Martin Robertson.

Norton, Philip (1985), 'Introduction', in Philip Norton (ed.), *Parliament in the 1980s*, Oxford: Basil Blackwell.

Norton, Philip (1996), 'The United Kingdom: Political Conflict, Parliamentary Scrutiny', in Philip Norton (ed.), *National Parliaments and the European Union*, London: Frank Cass.

Norton, Philip (2001), 'Playing by the Rules: The Constraining Hand of Parliamentary Procedure', *The Journal of Legislative Studies*, Vol. 7 (3): 13–33.

Norton, Philip (2007a), 'Adding Value? The Role of Second Chambers', *Asia Pacific Law Review*, Vol. 15 (1), 3–18.

Norton, Philip (2007b), 'The Constitution', in Anthony Seldon (ed.), *Blair's Britain 1997–2007*, Cambridge: Cambridge University Press.

Norton, Philip (2011a), 'Reform of the House of Lords', The Stevenson Lecture, University of Glasgow.

Norton, Philip (2011b), 'Introduction: A Century of Change', *Parliamentary History*, Vol. 30 (1), pp. 1–18.

Norton, Philip (2013), 'Parliament Act 1911 in its Historical Context', in David Feldman (ed.), *Law in Politics, Politics in Law*, Oxford: Hart Publishing.

Norton, Philip (2015), 'The Coalition and the Conservatives', in Anthony Seldon and Mike Finn (eds), *The Coalition Effect 2010–2015*, Cambridge: Cambridge University Press.

Norton, Philip (2016), 'Legislative Scrutiny in the House of Lords', in Alexander Horne and Andrew Le Seuer (eds), *Parliament: Legislation and Accountability*, Oxford: Hart Publishing.

Ostrogorski, Moisei (1902), *Democracy and the Organisation of Political Parties*, Vol. 1, London: Macmillan.

Perceval, R. W. (1954), 'The Origin and Development of the House of Lords', in Sydney D. Bailey (ed.), *The Future of the House of Lords*, London: The Hansard Society.

Pitkin, Hannah (1967), *The Concept of Representation*, Berkeley CA: University of California Press.

Public Administration Committee, House of Commons (2002), *The Second Chamber: Continuing the Reform*, 5th Report, Session 2001–2, HC 494-I.

Riddell, Peter (1993), *Honest Opportunism*, London: Hamish Hamilton.

Riddell, Peter (1995), 'The Impact of the Rise of the Career Politician', *The Journal of Legislative Studies*, Vol. 1, 186–91.

Rowland, Peter (1968), *The Last Liberal Government*, New York: Macmillan Company.

Royal Commission on the Constitution (1973), *Report of the Royal Commission on the Constitution*, Cmnd 5470, London: Her Majesty's Stationery Office.

Royal Commission on the Reform of the House of Lords (2000), *A House for the Future*, Cm. 4534, London: The Stationery Office.

Russell, Meg (2000), *Reforming the House of Lords: Lessons from Overseas*, Oxford: Oxford University Press.

Russell, Meg (2007), 'Peers' and Public Attitudes to the Contemporary House of Lords', *Briefing for a Seminar in the House of Lords, 12 Dec. 2007*, London: The Constitution Unit.

Russell, Meg (2013), *The Contemporary House of Lords*, Oxford: Oxford University Press.

Russell, Meg, Morris, Bob and Larkin, Phil (2013), *Fitting the Bill: Bringing Commons legislation committees into line with best practice*, London: The Constitution Unit.

Sacks, Lord (2012), Evidence, *Joint Committee on the Draft House of Lords Reform Bill: Report*, Vol. III, Session 2012–13, HL Paper 284-III, HC 1313-III: 175–8.

Shell, Donald (2007), *The House of Lords*, 2nd edn, Manchester: Manchester University Press.

Society of Conservative Lawyers (1978), *House of Lords Reform?* London: Macmillan.

Tyler, Colin (2012), Evidence, *Joint Committee on the Draft House of Lords Reform Bill: Report*, Vol. III, Session 2012–13, HL Paper 284-III, HC 1313-III: 200.

Weston, Corinne Comstock (1986), 'Salisbury and the Lords, 1868–1895', in Clyve Jones and David Lewis Jones (eds), *Peers, Politics and Power: The House of Lords 1603–1911*, London: The Hambledon Press.

Wilson, Harold (1971), *The Labour Government 1964–1970*, London: Weidenfeld & Nicolson/Michael Joseph.

Winterton, George (1979), 'Is the House of Lords Immortal?' *Law Quarterly Review*, Vol. 95: 386–92.

Wyndham, William (1998), *Peers in Parliament Reformed*, London: Quiller Press.

Index